320.5
SPA

P9-DCU-917

access to history

themes

SOCIALISM *and* COMMUNISM

Roger Spalding

Hodder & Stoughton

A MEMBER OF THE HODDER HEADLINE GROUP

Acknowledgements

The publishers would like to thank the following for permission to use copyright illustrations: The National Museum of Labour History, p.48, p.78; Topham Picture Point, p.62; Bildarchiv Preussischer Kulturbesitz, p. 69; David King Collection, p. 99; Tony Benn, p, 128.

The publishers would like to thank the following for permission to reproduce material in the volume:Addison Wesley Longman Ltd for an extract from Sidney and Beatrice Webb, *Soviet Communism: A New Civilisation?* 1935, p.602, and for an extract from Stephen Padgett and William E. Paterson, *A History of Social Democracy in Post-War Europe*, 1991, p.258; Andre Deutsch for an extract from Sebastian Haffner, *Failure of a Revolution. Germany 1918-19*, 1973, p.65; Harper Collins Publishers for an extract from Dimitri Volkogonov, *Lenin. Legacy and Life*, 1994, pp.155-6, and for an extract from Alan Bullock, *Hitler and Stalin: Parallel Lives*, 1991, p.190, and for an extract from Jung Chang, *Wild Swans*, 1993, p.129, and for an extract from Michael Foot, *Aneurin Bevan 1945-1960*, 1982, p.638; Lawrence and Wishart for an extract from Mao Zedong, Analysis of the Classes in Chinese Society in *Selected Works of Mao Zedong Vol 1*, 1954, p.14, and for an extract from Mao Zedong, Strategic Problems of China's Revolutionary War in *Selected Works of Mao Zedong Vol 1*, 1954, p.244; Little, Brown & Company (UK) for an extract from John Rentoul, *Tony Blair*, 1996, p.357; Macmillan Publishers Ltd for an extract from David McLellan, *Marxism After Marx*, 1980, p.72, and for an extract from E.H. Carr, *The Twilight of the Comintern 1930-1935*, 1982, p.373, and for an extract from Geoffrey Foote, *The Labour Party's Political Thought*, 1997, p.328; Moshe Lewin for an extract from *Lenin's Last Struggle*, Faber and Faber, 1969, pp. 139-40; The Orion Publishing Group Ltd for an extract from David Caute, *The Left in Europe Since 1789*, 1966; Oxford University Press for an extract from Peter Singer, *Marx*, 1980, p.60, and for an extract from Leonid Brezhnev in Gale Stokes (ed.), *From Stalinism to Pluralism*, 1991, p.133; Penguin UK for an extract from Karl Marx, Friedrich Engels, *The Communist Manifesto*, 1967, and for an extract from Edmund Wilson, *To the Finland Station*, 1991, and for an extract from Boris Nicolaievsky, Otto Maenchen-Helfen, *Karl Marx: Man and Fighter*, 1976, and for an extract from David Fernbach (ed.), *Marx. The First International and After*, 1974, p.48, and for an extract from Walter Kendall, *The Labour Movement in Europe*, 1975, p.104, and for an extract from Isaac Deutscher, *Stalin*, 1966, p.328, and for an extract from Stuart Schram, *Mao Tse-tung*, 1975, p.220; Pelican Publishing Company for an extract from Karl Marx, *Economic and Philosophical Manuscripts of 1844* in Lucio Colletti (ed.) *Early Writings. Marx*, 1974, p.235; Pluto Press for an extract from Gregor Benton (ed.), *Wild Lilies and Poisonous Weeds. Dissident Voices From People's China*, 1982, p.41, and for an extract from J.T. Murphy, *Preparing for Power*, 1972, p.37; Random House UK Ltd for an extract from C.A.R. Crosland, *The Future of Socialism*, 1956, pp.151-29; Routledge for an extract from W.L. Guttsman, *The German Social Democratic Party 1875-1933*, 1981, p.319, and for an extract from Alan Wood, *Stalin and Stalinism*, 1990, p.34; Schocken Books for an extract from C.A.R. Crosland, *The Conservative Enemy*, 1962; I.B. Tauris & Co Ltd for an extract from Donald Sassoon, *One Hundred Years of Socialism*, 1997, p.262-3; Thames and Hudson Ltd for an extract from W.T. Rogers (ed.), *Hugh Gaitskell 1906-1960*, 1964, p.126; University of California Press for extracts from James R. Townsend, *Political Participation in Communist China*, 1969, p.67.

Every effort has been made to trace and acknowledge ownership of copyright. The publishers will be glad to make any suitable arrangements with copyright holders whom it has not been possible to contact.

British Library Cataloguing in Publication Data
A catalogue for this title is available from the British Library

ISBN 0 340 72504 4

First published 1999

Impression number	10	9	8	7	6	5	4	3	2	1
Year			2004	2003	2002	2001	2000	1999		

Copyright © 1999 Roger Spalding

All rights reserved. No part of this publication may be reproduced or transmitted in any form or by any means, electronic or mechanical, including photocopy, recording, or any information storage and retrieval system, without permission in writing from the publisher or under licence form the Copyright Licensing Agency Limited. Further details of such licences (for reprographic reproduction) may be obtained from the Copyright Licensing Agency Limited, 90 Tottenham Court Road, London W1P 9HE.

Cover photo shows 'Friendship of the People's' by I. Karpov, reproduced courtesy of Novosti (London).

Typeset by Sempringham publishing services, Bedford
Printed in Great Britain for Hodder & Stoughton Educational,
a division of Hodder Headline Plc, 338 Euston Road, London NW1 3BH
by Redwood Books, Trowbridge, Wiltshire.

Contents

Preface

The original *Access to History* series was conceived as a collection of sets of books covering popular chronological periods in British history, such as 'the Tudors' and 'the nineteenth century', together with the histories of other countries, such as France, Germany, Russia and the USA. This arrangement complemented the way in which early modern and modern history has traditionally been taught in sixth forms, colleges and universities. In recent years, however, other ways of dividing up the past have become increasingly popular. In particular, there has been a greater emphasis on studying relatively brief periods in considerable detail and on comparing similar historical phenomena in different countries. These developments have generated a demand for appropriate learning materials, and, in response, two new 'strands' are being added to the main series - *In Depth* and *Themes*. The new volumes build directly on the features that have made *Access to History* so popular.

To the general reader

Although *Access* books have been specifically designed to meet the needs of examination students, these volumes also have much to offer the general reader. *Access* authors are committed to the belief that good history must not only be accurate, up-to-date and scholarly, but also clearly and attractively written. The main body of the text (excluding the 'Study Guides') should, therefore, form a readable and engaging survey of a topic. Moreover, each author has aimed not merely to provide as clear an explanation as possible of what happened in the past but also to stimulate readers and to challenge them into thinking for themselves about the past and its significance. Thus, although no prior knowledge is expected from the reader, he or she is treated as an intelligent and thinking person throughout. The author tends to share ideas and explore possibilities, instead of delivering so-called 'historical truths' from on high.

To the student reader

It is intended that *Access* books should be used by students studying history at a higher level. Its volumes are all designed to be working texts, which should be reasonably clear on a first reading but which will benefit from re-reading and close study. To be an effective and successful student, you need to budget your time wisely. Hence you should think carefully about how important the material in a particular book is for you. If you simply need to acquire a general grasp of a topic, the following approach will probably be effective:

1. Read Chapter 1, which should give you an overview of the whole book, and think about its contents.

2. Skim through Chapter 2, paying particular attention to the opening section and to the headings and sub-headings. Decide if you need to read the whole chapter.
3. If you do, read the chapter, stopping at the end of every sub-division of the text to make notes.
4. Repeat stage 2 (and stage 3 where appropriate) for the other chapters.

If, however, your course - and your particular approach to it - demands a detailed knowledge of the contents of the book, you will need to be correspondingly more thorough. There is no perfect way of studying, and it is particularly worthwhile experimenting with different styles of note-making to find the one that best suits you. Nevertheless, the following plan of action is worth trying:

1. Read a whole chapter quickly, preferably at one sitting. Avoid the temptation - which may be very great - to make notes at this stage.
2. Study the flow diagram at the end of the chapter, ensuring that you understand the general 'shape' of what you have read.
3. Re-read the chapter more slowly, this time taking notes. You may well be amazed at how much more intelligible and straightforward the material seems on a second reading - and your notes will be correspondingly more useful to you when you have to write an essay or revise for an exam. In the long run, reading a chapter twice can, in fact, often save time. Be sure to make your notes in a clear, orderly fashion, and spread them out so that, if necessary, you can later add extra information.
4. Read the advice on essay questions, and do tackle the specimen titles. (Remember that if learning is to be effective, it must be active. No one - alas - has yet devised any substitute for real effort. It is up to you to make up your own mind on the key issues in any topic.)
5. Attempt the source-based questions. The guidance on tackling these exercises, which is generally given at least once in a book, is well worth reading and thinking about.

When you have finished the main chapters, go through the 'Further Reading' section. Remember that no single book can ever do more than introduce a topic, and it is to be hoped that - time permitting - you will want to read more widely. If *Access* books help you to discover just how diverse and fascinating the human past can be, the series will have succeeded in its aim - and you will experience that enthusiasm for the subject which, along with efficient learning, is the hallmark of all the best students.

Robert Pearce

1 Introduction: Defining Socialism

1 Introduction

Radical movements demanding social reform have occurred throughout history. Prior to the Industrial Revolution such movements tended to focus on the issue of access to the land for farming, and often supported their claims with religious arguments.

Industrialisation moved the focus of radical movements towards the newly created industrial working class. Access to the land ceased to be the central issue and was replaced by conflicts over the distribution of items of consumption. Broadly speaking, it was argued that workers produced everything, but were paid only a fraction of the value of what they made. Socialism - the term was first used in 1827 - would, it was claimed, produce a society of plenty, a society in which workers would enjoy the full benefits of what they produced. Socialism, then, was a radical movement that based its arguments primarily on economics, rather than religion. This stress on equal access to the products of society was a common feature of all the socialist movements that emerged, principally in Britain and France, in the first 30 years of the 19th century.

In the early 19th century socialism had at most a handful of followers often engaged in trying to establish their own co-operative communities. Yet by the end of the century socialism was an international movement which, far from developing isolated independent communities, was actively engaged in the struggle for political power. By 1898, for example, the German Social Democratic Party (SPD), formed in 1875, held 56 seats in the Imperial German Parliament (Reichstag), and received two million votes. In the next 14 years these figures increased to 110 seats and 4.5 million votes, thus making it the largest single party in the Reichstag.

The first half of the 20th century saw even more dramatic advances. By 1950 many Western European states, including Britain, had experienced periods of socialist government; all of the states of Eastern Europe had communist governments; and two massive communist regimes, in the shape of the USSR and the People's Republic of China (PRC), dominated much of the land mass of Asia. At that point it certainly seemed that socialism, or rather its communistic form, was advancing throughout the world; indeed, American foreign policy for much of the post-war period was directed towards halting this advance.

In more recent times, however, this perceived threat has entirely vanished, with the collapse of the Soviet Union and the communist regimes of Eastern Europe. Socialism is no longer 'the hope of the world', as it was proclaimed in the 19th century. Even those socialist parties that still retain power - organisations as diverse as the British Labour Party and the Communist Party of China (CCP) - are enthusiastically embracing free market economics and abandoning the specifically socialist elements of their heritage.

Socialism may, at present, be a declining force, but it nevertheless remains of interest to the historian because of the massive impact it has had on political and social developments, particularly in the 20th century.

Yet studying socialism/communism as an international movement does present certain problems and these we must consider.

i) The first problem is that of the precise relationship between socialism and communism. In the early 19th century, according to George Licteim, communism had three distinct features: its followers were overwhelmingly working class in origin; they were committed to the radical and equal redistribution of property; and they believed in the need for a revolutionary dictatorship in the immediate aftermath of the socialist revolution.[1] Although it was given a particular ideological form by Marx and Engels, these three elements continued to be key aspects of communism right through to the Bolshevik Revolution of 1917. Communists were/are socialists committed to a specific form of socialism, and a particular method of bringing it into existence. In the period after the Bolshevik Revolution, the entire socialist movement was polarised into two frequently hostile blocs as a consequence of these differences.

ii) From this flows a second problem, which is how to define socialism. Here, even among non-communist socialists, the same two points of contention emerge: what will be the essential features of the new socialist society, and how will it be brought into existence? Widely differing views on these issues can be found within parties as much as between them. Tony Benn, for example, a key left-wing figure in the Labour Party, particularly prominent in the early 1980s, sees the public ownership of the principal components of the national economy as a central element of socialism.[2] Tony Blair, the leader of the Labour Party, simply rejects ' ... the old debates between public or private sector, market or state', in favour of 'a new agenda'.[3] Differences also existed between the 19th-century socialist pioneers. Sidney Webb, a founding members of the Fabian Society, for example, believed that Britain would move gradually towards socialism as a consequence of the legislation enacted by the Liberal and Conservative parties, whereas the socialist designer and writer, William Morris, argued for a social revolution, by which he meant a sudden and complete change from private to social ownership.

iii) Morris took his politics from the writings of Karl Marx, and, indeed, Marxism represents the most fully developed theory of socialism that we have. Unfortunately, the language of Marxism, both in the original works and in academic commentaries, is often difficult to follow. Another problem is that the student is not confronted with one Marxism but with a whole variety. Political conflict within 20th-century Marxist movements has spawned a number of 'isms': Leninism, Stalinism, Trotskyism, Maoism, and so on. Which of these represents the 'correct' interpretation of Marx's doctrine is almost impossible to decide, but the existence of these different political tendencies does present the history student with the problem of explaining their development.

iv) From its earliest days socialism has been an internationalist movement. This was based on the belief that the working people of all countries had a common interest in opposing their exploitative, owning classes. Hence the famous rallying cry of the *Communist Manifesto*: 'Working Men of All Countries, Unite!'[4]

Inspired by this internationalism there were several attempts, beginning in 1864 with the International Working Men's Association, or First International, to establish international organisations to link working class and socialist movements around the world. However, the experience of the Internationals soon demonstrated that despite their internationalism socialist movements were greatly influenced and shaped by their national traditions and loyalties. Hence, the Socialist International (also known as the Second International, founded in 1889) passed a great many anti-war resolutions, stressing the brotherhood of all workers, but it was nevertheless shattered in August 1914, when the great majority of the national parties supported their governments in the war that broke out in that month. The internationalism of the European socialist movement was, in actuality, a question of conference resolutions. In practice national loyalties always prevailed over theoretical commitments to internationalism. Students of socialism as an international movement have, therefore, always to take account of specific national factors.

v) The issue of internationalism took another turn after the formation of the Communist International (Comintern, in Russian usage) or Third International in 1919. This organisation was founded by the victorious Bolsheviks and based in Moscow. It sought to co-ordinate the activities of the communist parties that were formed around the world in the wake of the Russian Revolution. Inspired by their victory, Soviet communists imposed their methods and forms of organisation on all of the parties affiliated to the Communist International.

1 The Communist International considers the dictatorship of the proletariat the only possible way to liberate mankind from the horrors of capitalism. And the Communist International considers the Soviet power [to be] the historically given form of this dictatorship of the
5 proletariat.[5]

This approach, it has been argued, had the effect of imposing inappropriate methods on all of the new communist parties, especially those in democratic states. The authoritarian party structures which were appropriate for operating illegally in Tsarist Russia sometimes alienated potential recruits, brought up in more open Western societies. Stalin's assumption of absolute power in the late 1920s further complicated the situation, as the Communist International rapidly degenerated into an arm of Soviet foreign policy. At the very least, then, the link with the Soviet Union distorted the contribution of communist parties to the development of socialism. The dramatic policy turns imposed upon the communist parties tended to undermine their credibility. In 1929, for example, communists were ordered to denounce social democrats as 'social fascists', and yet in 1935 they were instructed to construct anti-fascist alliances with them. These policy changes, combined with a completely uncritical attitude to the Soviet Union, made many socialists deeply suspicious of the communist parties.

vi) The final problem to consider is that of parties and movements that use the term socialism in an apparently inappropriate way. Iraq, for example, is ruled by the Ba'ath Socialist Party. However, it is very difficult to see how a regime presided over by an unelected dictator and his family coterie, all living in great luxury while most of the Iraqi people endure severe shortages of basic goods, can be described as socialist in any sense at all. The most significant example of this apparent misuse is the National Socialist German Workers' Party - better known as the Nazi Party. Hitler loathed Marxism, and physically destroyed all German socialist parties. In what sense, then, was he a socialist ?

Democratic politicians are not above misusing the term as well. In Britain many Conservative politicians, particularly in the immediate post-war period, regularly referred to the Labour Party as 'The Socialist Party'. Their intention here was clearly to make Labour seem more radical than it was, and to link the Party to the 'socialist' regimes emerging in Eastern Europe at this time.

Students can be daunted by the number of 'isms' confronting them when studying socialism/communism. Attempting to define Leninism and Trotskyism as static doctrines is difficult. However, history is concerned with movement and development, and such an approach, by placing doctrines in their political and chronological context, makes it much easier to understand their distinctive elements. Or, to take another example, Maoism is much easier to understand if students can see its development as linked to the practical problems the CCP faced in its struggle for power before 1949.

There is also no need for the ideas of Marxism to be expressed in inaccessible language. If, as it is claimed, Marxism is a coherent and logical system, then it should be possible to convey its central ideas in a clear and straightforward manner. This book seeks to provide an understanding of the development of socialist and communist ideas that will enable students to appreciate the role played by these movements in shaping the modern world

2 Fundamental Questions

Socialist have argued about the nature of socialism for at least 160 years. These discussions have produced a multiplicity of definitions and fierce disagreements between supporters of rival definitions. Clearly, in a book of this size, it is impossible to explore all the available definitions. Consequently, in order to produce a coherent overview of the development of socialism, it is crucial that clear and precise questions are formulated about the nature of the doctrine.

i) **What are the common roots of socialism and communism?**

It is clear that the title of this book is based upon the belief that socialism and communism have a close relationship. That this was not an easy relationship is demonstrated by the fact that while communists were/are quite happy to describe themselves as socialists, the vast majority of socialists are not willing to describe themselves as communists. The need to identify accurately the exact nature of the links between communism and socialism flows, to some extent, from the efforts of Conservative critics to present them as essentially the same.

ii) **What are the reasons for the divergence between communism and socialism?**

This second question follows from the first, because if these movements have common roots, they must have moved in different directions at some point. There is an obvious point of divergence that began with the First World War and ended with the Bolshevik Revolution of 1917. This was a divergence between those who supported their national governments in the war and those who saw the war as being fought solely in the interests of the owning classes, and who consequently refused to support it. However, it is possible to find much earlier evidence of antagonism between these movements. In 1848, for example, the pioneer English socialist, Robert Owen, attacked 'Red Republicans, Communists and Socialists of Europe' whose policies, he claimed, led to 'universal disunion, opposition, competition ... a pandemonium state of society'.[6] In the same year the Communist, Karl Marx, described Owen as a 'utopian socialist', by which he meant that Owen's ideas were impractical and bore little relationship to the realities of contemporary politics.[7] The enduring nature of the controversy between socialists and communists would suggest that it is based upon a key, defining point of principle, the investigation of which could shed considerable light on the nature of these varieties of socialism.

iii) **Why have communists only achieved power in relatively undeveloped states?**

According to Karl Marx the revolution that would initiate the process of moving towards communism would be the work of the proletariat, or industrial working class. He also argued that such revolutions would occur first in the most developed capitalist states. In such countries the working class would constitute the majority of the population and the economy would be sufficiently developed to ensure conditions of material plenty after the revolution. In the event, however, communists have gained power only in underdeveloped states with tiny proletariats, states such as Russia, China, Cuba, Vietnam. At one level this might be seen to call into question key aspects of Marx's theory. For whatever reason the workers in developed capitalist countries have not achieved a sufficiently high level of class consciousness to opt for revolutionary change. Could this be because, by and large, such economies have satisfied, rather than denied, the wants and needs of their workers? On the other hand it could equally be argued that communism has never been tried in a situation where the conditions for it were right. It is also interesting to note that social democracy has achieved power only in developed Western societies. This would seem to indicate a clear relationship between the development of political democracy and the forms that radical movements take.

iv) **Is communism the same as fascism?**

Since the Second World War a number of analysts have argued that communist and fascist regimes were essentially the same in character. They labelled such regimes 'totalitarian', a term that referred to the attempts by single-party governments, using a variety of methods such as political indoctrination and repression exercised through secret police forces, to control all aspects of the lives of their citizens. Such analysts also point to the domination of totalitarian states by all-powerful dictators, for example Hitler, Stalin, Mao Zedong. In the early 1940s it was suggested that totalitarianism represented the next stage of political/social organisation, after capitalism. George Orwell's novel, *Nineteen Eighty-Four*, was based on this view. In the Cold War era the term was used, predominantly, to describe communist regimes and, thereby, to illustrate their negative features in relation to the democracies. In other words, this was not a precise term, as its meaning changed as the political context changed. As a concept it also failed to account for key differences between communism and fascism, or to account for their mutual and fundamental antagonism. Nevertheless it is an idea that has to be seriously considered because of the influence that it continues to exercise on Western thought.

v) **Is socialism compatible with electoral politics?**

Since its inception in 1900 the Labour Party has accepted that power can only be achieved through elections. In 1918 the Party adopted a socialist constitution which appeared to commit it to bringing the bulk of the economy into state ownership. Despite enjoying periods of office since 1918, the Labour Party has never attempted to take over the economy as a whole. Indeed, by the early 1960s a serious effort was made to abandon the nationalisation clause - Clause 4 - of the constitution. In 1962 a prominent party member described nationalisation as a 'political liability'.[8] Nor was this attitude confined to Great Britain; in the late 1950s the German Social Democratic Party (SPD) formally abandoned its Marxist programme. For many years the Marxism of the SPD had been a dead letter, but its abandonment signalled to the world that, like the British Labour Party, it sought not to transform property relationships but merely to manage efficiently an existing mixed (capitalist) economy.

In following this course the British and German socialists were taking their lead from the Socialist International, to which many socialist parties were affiliated. In the early 1950s the International declared that socialist planning 'does not presuppose public ownership of all the means of production'.[9] In more recent times (March 1998) Tony Blair, leader of the Labour Party, declared in a speech to the French National Assembly that there is no left or right in economic policy, there are only policies that work. As Blair has rejected the idea of socialist transformation, 'working' must mean successfully operating a profit-making capitalist economy. It would seem possible, then, that 20th-century socialist parties have decided to abandon socialist commitments as a perceived necessary step towards electoral success.

vi) **What is the relationship of Social Democracy to socialism?**

Social Democracy is a term that has experienced a dramatic change of meaning over the years. Originally, it was a term used by 19th- and early 20th-century Marxists. Hence, before 1917 Lenin and the Bolsheviks described themselves as Social Democrats. After the First World War revolutionary Marxists abandoned the term because it was, in their eyes, tainted with support for the war effort and with an abandonment of Marxism. In this period it came to mean socialists who were committed to parliamentary methods. As a consequence of this change of meaning the term was sometimes used to describe the British Labour Party, although this had never been a Marxist party. After the Second World War the term, largely because of the changes in the German SPD, increasingly became associated with those socialists most identified with the ideas of economic management in a mixed economy, rather than nationalisation. Hugh Gaitskell's attempt, when Labour leader, to abandon Clause 4 in the early 1960s was very much a product of social democratic thinking. The majority of those who split away from Labour in the early 1980s to form the Social Democratic Party (SDP) were originally Gaitskellite socialists. So the relationship of social democracy to socialism varies according to the historical context within which the term is used.

vii) **Is socialism finished as a political movement?**

Given what has been said above about the development of socialism, and given the collapse of communism across Eastern Europe, it seems that there is a great deal of evidence for the death of socialism. One American analyst has argued that history is at an end because the world-wide victory of liberal-democratic capitalism means that there will be no more ideological conflicts between rival social systems.[10] It is always dangerous to make predictions. Indeed, that is not the task of the historian. However, it seems very unlikely that communism or socialism will experience a revival in the shape of the old socialist and communist parties. It does seem safe to predict though that major inequalities will continue to exist within all societies, and that such inequalities potentially have the power to generate new forms of socialism, or something like it.

viii) **How do we define socialism?**

It is, of course, possible to find dictionary definitions of socialism. These are not, however, very helpful: they are static and give little insight into the role of socialism at any specific point in history. Definitions of socialism change over time and according to national circumstances. Therefore the only way to approach the issue of definition is by providing a brief historical outline.

3 Socialism: A General Outline

a) The Development of Socialism

In the early 19th century socialism tended to mean a belief in a society in which workers received the full value of what they produced. Early socialists attempted to establish such a society through the creation of small, self-sufficient communities that consumed what they produced, or bartered with similar communities. This programme for the peaceful replacement of capitalism was opposed by those who sought to overthrow the existing order using revolutionary methods. This communist tradition began with Babeuf's organisation, the Conspiracy of Equals, in late 18th-century France (see page 21). The distinction between communism and socialism was clarified by Marx and Engels in the late 1840s, when they developed a theory of political change - Marxism - that was based on the belief in the necessity of progress through revolution. The full significance of the distinction, however, only became apparent after the Bolshevik Revolution of 1917.

In the last 25 years of the 19th century, industrialisation, combined with periodic booms and slumps in the international economy, created the conditions for major gains for the socialists. The most important European party to emerge in this period was the German Social Democratic Party (SPD). The size and the success of this Marxist party - at this point, of course, Social Democrat meant Marxist - enabled it to impose its will on other European socialist parties through the medium of the Socialist International. Affiliated parties were to commit themselves to the ultimate goal of socialist revolution, maintain their independence from their national ruling classes and, on a day-to-day basis, engage in 'political' activities, by which was meant electoral politics. In effect electoral activity came to figure much more prominently than preparations for the distant revolutionary goal. This emphasis made it perfectly possible for non-Marxist organisations, like the Independent Labour party (ILP) and, later, the Labour party, to participate in the work of the International.

Other parties in the International, in particular the Bolshevik wing of the Russian Social Democratic Labour Party (RSDLP), took their revolutionary commitments more seriously, largely because the autocratic Russian state offered few electoral opportunities. When war broke out in 1914, instead of supporting the national government, as most socialist parties did, the Bolsheviks called for its defeat. Catapulted into power by the October Revolution of 1917, the Bolsheviks changed their name to the Communist Party and split the international socialist movement by establishing revolutionary communist parties throughout the world, all affiliated to a new Communist International. Broadly speaking, the new communist parties confronted socialist parties that were increasingly committed to reforming the worse excesses of capitalism, whatever their constitutions said, not totally overthrowing it as a system. In this situation the term 'Social Democratic' took on an entirely new meaning; consequently it became possible to describe the British Labour Party - an organisation that at no point subscribed to Marxism - as a social democratic party.[11]

The development of the world communist movement was intimately bound up with events in the Soviet Union. With the consolidation of Stalin's position at the head of the Soviet state, the movement increasingly became a tool of his foreign policy. Communist parties found themselves forced to make dramatic and sometimes disastrous policy changes, and to defend every aspect of Soviet society. In the depressed inter-war years many were prepared to do this, believing that the Soviet Union was immune from the failures of capitalist society and was leading the way to the future.

In the post-Second World War period the tide of communist advance - in Western Europe, at least - began to recede. The brutalities inflicted on the peoples of Eastern Europe, particularly the suppression of the 1956 Hungarian uprising, and the information that began to reach the West about the nature of Stalin's political methods, caused many to leave the communist parties. In the early 1960s some of these dissidents switched their allegiance to Mao's China. The Chinese had fallen out with the Russians and had begun to criticise their erstwhile comrades' lack of revolutionary commitment. However, Mao's peasant-based revolution had little to offer as a model to communists in industrial states. Other ex-communists joined the small Trotskyist groupings scattered around the world. In 1938 Trotsky, expelled from the Soviet Union, had established the Fourth International to keep alive the idea of world revolution, and weld together the small groups of his supporters. In the event the Trotskyists have only attracted a minimal following, and have been divided into a handful of sects quarrelling over minute points of principle.

Eastern Europe aside, the most successful form of socialism in the period after 1945 was social democracy. In Britain, Scandinavia and Germany such parties created welfare states and intervened extensively in their national economies. So successful were these parties that high levels of welfare spending became the norm in the post-war world, accepted by may, if not most, non-socialists. One of the problems of post-war social democracy was its emphasis on the citizen as consumer. As their policies improved standards of living, they simultaneously eroded the class solidarity that had originally led to their formation. To put it simply, the trade unionist living on a council estate may well support extensive welfare programmes. The same trade unionist, a successful skilled worker perhaps, living in the suburbs as a homeowner and possessor of a range of consumer goods, car, etc., may well be much more interested in low rates of income tax.

When the post-war political consensus - a general agreement on welfare, employment and economic policies - collapsed in the late 1970s European social democrats were forced to reorientate themselves. The rejuvenated forms of social democracy that emerged in the 1990s placed a much greater emphasis on market forces and were less willing to fund extensive welfare systems.

If nothing else this brief survey should have demonstrated that since its first appearance socialism has taken a variety of forms, and that changing historical and national circumstances are the key factors behind such changes. To take one example, in the depressed circumstances of the 1930s the English socialists, Sidney and Beatrice Webb, neither of them Marxists, declared that Soviet Russia was a new civilisation. The Webbs impressed by the apparent absence of unemployment and the seeming success of economic planning, made very favourable comparisons between dynamic Soviet society and declining Western capitalist society. In the post-war period of economic growth, however, when the terrible cost in human life of

Soviet industrialisation became known, the attitudes of many Western socialists changed dramatically, and they became distinctly pro-American in outlook. So socialism and perceptions of socialism change over time. But how does this help us to define socialism?

b) Preliminary Definitions

All forms of socialism are concerned with the need to achieve a fairer, more equal distribution of goods and services. However, that apparently simple aspiration raises two further questions: how is this to be brought about, and what will the new socialist society look like? The different forms of socialism stem from different answers to these questions. Some socialists argue the need for revolutionary change; other believe that change should come through elections. Some socialists argue that state management of a largely privately owned economy is the way to social justice.

Another complicating factor is that socialism, unlike fascism, in its classical form is still a live movement. It is not simply a movement of the past that can be studied in a detached way. Many of those who write about socialism are actively engaged in socialist politics of one form or another. Hence, an established academic political scientist argues:

1   The abolition of classes is possible only where capitalist relations of production [i.e. a privately owned economy run for profit] have lifted the productivity of labour to a level where scarcity can be abolished. We have seen how these relations come to act as a fetter on the produc-
5   tive forces, giving rise to a regular, cyclical succession of boom and slump.
    Another way of putting this is to say that capitalism makes communism possible and historically necessary.[12]

According to this account, capitalism is inherently crisis prone and must be replaced by communism, that is, by a society in which private property has been abolished. At about the same time as the above extract was written a leading British socialist politician argued:

1   We cannot resist change, but neither should we passively allow it to take its course. On the contrary, we should be the advocates of it, helping industry to modernise to meet its challenge, equipping both firms and people with the means to survive and prosper in a new and
5   highly competitive global market.[13]

In this account there is no intention to abolish private ownership: on the contrary, the author argues that governments should aid industry in its efforts to compete in the market place. Clearly both extracts are based on very different conceptions of socialism. The two extracts raise two important points. First, when reading about socialism it is often useful to know the views of the author; in this case the first author, Alex Callinicos, is an active Trotskyist; the second author is Tony Blair, the leader of the Labour Party. The second point is that what constitutes socialism is a matter of political choice. There is no right and wrong definition of socialism, but there are many different political interpretations of socialism.

Beyond the broadest generalities, then, there is no all-encompassing definition of socialism; rather there are a great many socialisms, some more significant than others.

c) Assessment

Generally speaking historians accept that there are a great number of forms of socialism; there is even agreement on many of the features of these different forms. Controversy arises over the emphasis historians place on these features. For example, nobody would dispute the fact that for many years the communist parties of the world had a close relationship with the Soviet Union. However, where official historians of the Communist Party of Great Britain, like Noreen Branson and James Klugmann, stress the value of such 'fraternal relationships', Henry Pelling, in his 1958 history of the CPGB, tends to portray British communists as 'dupes' of Moscow. Similarly, Pelling in his *Short History of the Labour Party* praises Labour's commitment to constitutional politics, while Ralph Miliband, in *Parliamentary Socialism*, argues that a commitment to electoral politics severely weakened Labour's commitment to socialism. All of these differences of interpretation flow, to a very large degree, from the political orientation of the authors. Students have to be aware that little of what they read in this area is, in any real sense, objective.

The best way to lessen subjective tendencies is to locate socialist movements within their historical contexts, seeing them develop in response to changing circumstances. This is what we shall attempt to do in the rest of this book. While it is very difficult for anybody to escape their own subjective views, it is to be hoped that this book will enable its readers to root their views in knowledge.

References

1   George Lichtheim, *A Short History of Socialism* (Fontana/Collins, 1970), p. 37.
2   Tony Benn, *Parliament, People and Power* (Verso, 1982), pp. 124-5.
3   Tony Blair, *Change and National Renewal. Leadership Election Statement* (Labour Party, 1994), p. 4.
4   Karl Marx and Friedrich Engels, *The Communist Manifesto* (Penguin, 1967), p. 4.
5   *Statutes of the Communist International* (Communist International, Moscow, 1920).
6   David Caute, *The Left in Europe Since 1789* (Weidenfeld and Nicolson, 1966), p. 37.

7   Marx and Engels, *Communist Manifesto*, pp. 117-8.
8   C.A.R. Crosland, *The Conservative Enemy* (Schocken Books, New York, 1962), p. 42.
9   Caute, *Left in Europe Since 1789*, p.43.
10 Francis Fukuyama, *The End of History and the Last Man* (Hamilton, 1992), p. 48.
11 David Howell, *British Social Democracy: A Study in Development and Decay* (Croom Helm, 1976).
12 Alex Callinicos, *The Revolutionary Ideas of Karl Marx* (Bookmarks, 1995), p. 160.
13 Blair, *Change and National Renewal*, p. 4.

Summary Diagram
Introduction: Defining Socialism

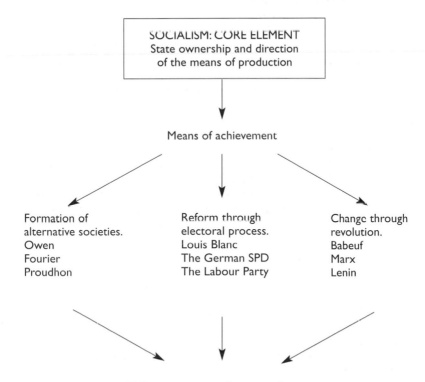

2 The Development of Socialist Theory 1800-1867

1 Introduction

Modern European socialism emerged in the early 19th century as a result of a number of related developments. In Britain the Industrial Revolution, beginning in the late 18th century, fundamentally changed the relationship between employer and employee. Previously labour relations had been governed by custom that determined mutually agreed rates of pay and working conditions. But as markets expanded employers found these customary practices a limitation on their ability to make profits. They began to base their labour relations on the 'laws' of supply and demand. In doing so they were following the ideas of a new school of political economists (or economists, as we would say today), who argued that commerce and industry should be freed from all customary and legal restrictions. This body of ideas became known as *laissez-faire*, which means 'let it alone'. The application of these ideas was felt by many workers to be against their interests. In Nottinghamshire in 1812 the stocking-knitters responded to the innovations of the employers with 'Luddism', a form of direct action that involved machine-breaking, armed attacks and assassinations, all with the aim of restoring earlier labour practices.

According to the historian E.P. Thompson, the significance of movements like 'Luddism' was that they demonstrated the emergence of a new working class that defined itself as being in opposition to the new industrialists and merchants. The importance of the term 'working class', as opposed to 'working classes', is that the latter simply means those who work and could therefore include employers, whereas the former term suggests a unity of reaction and response brought about by a recognition that the interests of employer and employee are fundamentally different. This conflict, for reasons recognised by Adam Smith, an 18th-century political economist, often involved the working class in opposition to the entire status quo.

> Civil government, so far as it is constituted for the security of property, is, in reality, instituted for the defence of the rich against the poor, or for those who have property against those who have none at all.[1]

Out of this conflict between capital and labour developed doctrines that challenged the individualistic and competitive outlook of the political economists. These new doctrines stressed co-operation and communal values, and formed the basis of what we know as socialism.

In France the Great Revolution (1789-94) profoundly altered social perceptions. It demonstrated that a social system could be overthrown by a mass revolutionary movement. It also demonstrated the conflict of social classes, firstly between the feudal classes (the aristocracy) and the *bourgeoisie*, or middle classes; and later between the *bourgeoisie* and the plebeian (lower class) *sans-culottes*, during the Reaction of 1795. Finally it popularised the idea that new societies could be constructed and run according to newly formulated principles, embodied in constitutions based on reason and logic rather than tradition.

The impact of these developments was not confined to France. Tom Paine's *The Rights of Man*, written to defend the French Revolution, was a best seller in late 18th-century Britain. Germany was also affected by the French Revolution. In territories that fell under French occupation during the Revolutionary Wars, the conquerors were greeted with considerable enthusiasm. Under French rule the restrictions of feudalism were removed, the power of the Church reduced, and the middle classes given greater opportunity for professional and commercial advancement. The restoration of royal control after 1815 saw the end of such radical developments. After that date critical thought was expressed in philosophical rather than open political debate.

These developments completely changed the way Western Europeans looked at society and their place within it. English Political Economy promoted an entirely new way of seeing the relationship between employer and employee. Labour was, according to this view, simply a commodity to be bought and sold, and whose price varied in relation to demand. French revolutionary politics transformed ideas of political change. The overthrow of the monarchy placed political authority in the hands of the people. The concept of popular sovereignty legitimised the idea of revolutionary social change as a form of democratic direct action.

In Germany the philosopher Hegel argued that history was a process of constant change. If such was true, no political regime could see itself as permanently secure. According to Lenin, these developments - English political economy, French revolutionary politics, German philosophy - were the 'three component parts of Marxism'. They also played a major part in the development of socialism in general.

2 Early English Socialism

Britain in the early 19th century experienced a period of social and economic turmoil. In the years 1799 and 1800 the government, fearful of revolution, passed the Combination Acts, banning trade unions. During the Luddite disturbances in 1812 the government felt the need to station 12,000 troops in the industrial counties to maintain order. The country was experiencing major economic change and, on top of this, was suffering the effects of over 20 years of warfare with France. Some working people turned to trade unionism, illegal until 1824; others, like the Luddites, used force in an attempt to restore their customary practices; and others tried to develop an analysis of society that would explain what was happening and point the way forward to a new type of society.

The first group of people to attempt this were the 'Ricardian-socialists'. The name came from their attempt to rework an aspect of David Ricardo's economic theory. In *The Wealth of the Nations* (1776), Adam Smith had argued that labour was the basis of all wealth.

> The property which every man has is his own labour, as it is the original of all other property, so it is the most sacred and inviolable.[2]

In other words, all wealth is the product of the application of labour. But, by this Smith, and later Ricardo, meant the labour of the industrialists and entrepreneur. In a series of lectures, later published as *Labour Defended Against the Claims of Capital* (1825), Thomas Hodgskin argued that it was the labour of the worker that was the source of all value. If this was the case, then, as the worker was only paid a fraction of the value of the goods produced, the economic system - capitalism - was in effect a form of institutionalised theft.

> 1 Betwixt him who produces clothing, betwixt him who makes instruments and him who uses them, in steps the capitalist, who neither makes them nor uses them, and appropriates to himself the produce of both. With as niggard a hand as possible he transfer to each part of the
> 5 produce of the other, keeping to himself the larger share ... While he despoils both, so completely does he exclude one from the view of the other that both believe they are indebted to him for subsistence ... I have shown it [capitalism] has no just claim to any share of the labourer's produce, and that what it actually receives is the cause of the
> 10 poverty of the labourer.[3]

The idea that the amount of labour incorporated in an object determined its value was to play a key part in the development of socialism. Marx, again using Ricardo, developed his own 'labour theory of value'. The 'labour theory of value' also played a central role in forming the ideas of Britain's most important early Socialist pioneer, Robert Owen.

a) Robert Owen

Owen (1771-1858) was apprenticed to a draper when he was ten. He became the manager of a Manchester cotton mill at the age of 20, and by the age of 30 was a wealthy millowner. Owen could be regarded as a classic self-made man, in a period that had many of them. However, Owen's experience of industrialisation led him to question the precepts normally used to justify it. He rejected the idea that labour was simply a commodity to be bought at the lowest possible price. He believed, on the contrary, that people could be decent only if they were treated decently and given decent living conditions. At his mills he provided schools for the children of his workers, provided good living and working conditions and, against the wisdom of the day that payment above the bare minimum spelt ruin, made a profit.

In his *Report to the County of Lanark* (1820), Owen accepted that labour was the source of all value. Following on from this he argued that capital - representing past labour - was best owned by the community and used co-operatively. By past labour he meant that all private wealth had originally been produced by the work of others. At this stage co-operation meant socialism. The earliest use of the term 'socialist' was in the Owenite *Co-operative Magazine* in 1827. Having decided that socialism represented the 'superior mode of forming character and creating wealth' that he desired, Owen now faced the task of how to bring it into existence. Initially he thought in terms of creating small co-operative communities. In the 1820s he attempted to establish 'Villages of Unity and Co-operation' as a way of dealing with unemployment. When this project failed he left for the United States, in 1824, and attempted to create a socialist community at the settlement of New Harmony.

In Owen's absence his ideas spread rapidly through the working population in Britain. In 1824 the London Co-operative Society was founded; this quickly established a store for the benefit of its members. The store enabled the Society to by-pass normal competitive trading, allowing members to engage in barter, and to accumulate funds for the setting up of co-operative communities. Owenite co-operation particularly appealed to independent skilled craftsmen, who were feeling the pressure of factory-based production. Groups of such men began to form small producers' co-operatives. The goods made by these were offered for sale in the stores of the co-operative societies. When Owen returned from the United States in 1829, he found a substantial movement bearing his name, a movement that by 1832 included 500 co-operative societies around the country.

Owen was particularly interested in the work of the producers' co-operatives. These groups seemed to offer the best opportunity for the development of a new social order. To encourage these societies he set up 'Labour Exchanges' in industrial centres. These exchanges provided a facility for the sale and barter of co-operatively produced goods. Within the Labour Exchanges goods were valued according to the cost price of the materials and the labour time involved in making them. The exchanges issued their own currency - Labour Notes - based on units of hours of labour. Most of the exchanges wound up in 1834, after two years of existence, overstocked with certain items and suffering shortages in other areas. This reflected the strengths and weaknesses of the co-operatives in their areas.

Owen's next major venture was the Grand National Consolidated Trade Union (GNCTU). This was not to be a conventional trade union: as well as being an umbrella group drawing together all of the various Owenite organisations, it was, more importantly, seen as the basis of an alternative form of government.

1 We have never yet had a House of Commons. The only House of Commons is a House of Trades and that is only just beginning to be formed. We shall have a new set of boroughs when the unions are organised; every trade shall be a borough, and every trade shall have a 5 council of representatives to conduct its affairs. Our present commoners know nothing of the interests of the people. They are all landholders. How can an employer represent a workman? There are 133,000 shoe-makers in the country, yet not one representative have they in the House of Commons. According to the proportion they bear 10 to the rest of the population they ought to have twenty-five representatives. The same is with the carpenters and other trades in proportion. Such a House of Commons, however, is growing.[4]

This analysis had a definite appeal to those working-class radicals who were disappointed by the 1832 Reform Act's failure to go beyond extending the franchise to the middle classes.

Within a few months of its formation in 1833, the GNCTU had a membership of over 500,000. The formation of the union produced a spate of strikes and lock-outs. In November 1833 employers in Derby presented their workers with 'the Document', a pledge renouncing union membership. The Great Derby Lock-out which subsequently ensued as workers refused to sign, and similar disputes around the country, seriously depleted the Union's funds.

As well as being financially damaging, these disputes revealed divisions within the leadership of the GNCTU. Owen, for example, had seen the GNCTU as a union of 'the well-disposed members of the industrious classes'. The 'industrious classes', in his view, included members of the middle class who had been convinced by the justice and logic of his co-operative vision. Others advocated a more militant, working-class union policy. Amidst these divisions and financial problems, the GNCTU was wound up in 1834. Thereafter Owen withdrew from active campaigning. His legacy was to be the Co-operative retail stores that developed up and down the country following the example of the Rochdale Pioneers Co-operative Society, which established the first such store in 1844. Ironically this was a movement that did not seek to replace capitalism, but to compete on behalf of its members within it, using conventional currency. Many other working-class Owenite activists turned their attention to the campaign for the People's Charter, seeking to gain working-class representation and social reform.

Karl Marx later characterised Owen as a 'utopian socialist'. By this he meant that Owen believed that he could formulate a plan for a perfect society, and then use it to convince people from all sections of society that it was the correct path to take. Hence, at the end of his work, *Book of the New Moral World*, Owen included a letter to King William IV.

> This book ... unfolds the fundamental principles of a *New Moral World*, and thus lays a new foundation on which to reconstruct change from this system, with all its evil consequences, to another founded on self-evident truths, ensuring happiness to all ...[5]

King William did not pledge himself to assist this endeavour. However, Owen was not alone in following the 'Utopian' path to socialism.

3 French Socialism

Between 1789 and 1851 France experienced three major revolutions. During this period France also underwent major economic changes. Industrialisation occurred on a smaller scale than in England, but it was nevertheless significant in certain areas. The various forms of socialism that appeared in France can, therefore, be seen as a product of this political and economic turmoil.

a) Henri de Saint-Simon

Saint-Simon (1760-1825) developed a model of society that combined religion with a recognition of the importance of science. In Saint-Simon's society there was to be a three-tiered hierarchy consisting of *savants*, the propertied, and the unpropertied. The *savants*, essentially the intellectuals, would provide the membership of the Council of Newton. Although this was the supreme body in Saint-Simon's society, it would not rule in a conventional sense. He envisaged that the artists and scientists of the Council would, by the production of new works of art and by making scientific discoveries, provide spiritual power for the rest of society. He used the name Newton because he had been told in a dream that God had selected the scientist Isaac Newton as the figure through whom he transmitted messages to humanity. The propertied class, in Saint-Simon's model, would undertake the work of government and the unpropertied would accept their role because it was in their best interests to do so.

Clearly the notion of equality played little part in Saint-Simon's thinking. His ideas, formulated in the early 19th century, are important in at least three respects. Firstly, Saint-Simon rejected the liberal individualism held by most 'advanced' thinkers of the time, and argued instead that society should be organised as a whole. Secondly, his stress on the supreme role of the 'expert' was passed down the years to modern socialist movements as diverse as the British Fabian Society (see page 46) and the Communist Party of the Soviet Union. Finally, his view that politics was primarily concerned with the production and consumption of goods would, later in the century, emerge in a more fully developed form in the works of Karl Marx.

b) Charles Fourier

The political doctrines of Fourier (1772-1837) read like a combination of Saint-Simon and Robert Owen. Fourier argued that the search for individual wealth was an anti-social activity that encouraged vice rather than virtue. In opposition to competitive society he sought to establish co-operative communities, which he called phalanxes. Within these communities differences in individual wealth would be acceptable as long as all wealth derived from co-operative effort. He also sought to invert the normal relationship between labour and capital. When income was distributed within the phalanxes four-twelfths was to go to capital, five-twelfths was to go to labour, and three-twelfths to talent. Fourier's politics were stimulated by his own experiences. He had seen, for example, the impoverishment of the citizens of Lyons, following the establishment of a modern textile industry. A desire to escape the consequences of industrialisation was probably the motivation behind the founding of 34 phalanxes in the United States during the first half of the 19th century. Like Owen's New Harmony these all failed, the victims of those who did not share, but were prepared to exploit, their aspirations.

c) Pierre-Joseph Proudhon

In 1840 Proudhon (1809-65) asked, in the title of his book, *What is Property?* His answer 'Property is Theft' has been misunderstood ever since. Proudhon did not believe that all property was theft, rather he believed that property which enabled its owner to live without working was theft. It was the property of the very rich that Proudhon objected to. Proudhon's politics reflected his background as a self-educated, independent craftsman. His ideal society was one made up of small-scale, independent communities co-operating together in a system that he called 'Mutualism'. This in turn reflected the predominantly peasant nature of French society and the small-scale nature of much of French industry. The social orientation of Proudhon's politics was made clear in his 1846 work, *System of Economic Contradiction, or the Philosophy of Poverty*. There he argued that the methods by which wealth circulated in society were more important than the methods of production. He further called for the establishment of banks that would lend money without interest. These proposals proved popular with France's peasant communities and with independent craftsmen. The lower middle class, struggling to improve its lot, was more prone to suffer at the hands of the banks than other social classes.

Proudhon was opposed to central governmental authority; in this he is seen as a pioneer of anarchism, with its belief that all forms of state authority are inevitably oppressive. At times Proudhon's opposition to central authority led him to adopt some strange positions. In 1861, for example, he came out in support of the slave-holding Confederate states in the American Civil War, on the basis that they were fighting against centralisation

In their various ways Proudhon, Fourier, and Saint-Simon attempted to respond to new political, social and economic conditions within France. Their approach was to formulate blueprints for their new societies. Their hope was that the logic of their proposals would of itself win supporters.

d) Babeuf and Blanqui

At least two other socialist traditions emerged in France in the early 19th century, the first of these was initiated by Gracchus Babeuf (1760-97). Babeuf was an activist and journalist in the French Revolution. In 1794 the regime headed by Robespierre was overthrown, initiating a backlash against the Jacobins. The Jacobins were the most radical faction involved in the Revolution. Babeuf opposed this development in the pages of his paper, *The Tribune of the People*. When this was suppressed he founded a political club, The Society of Equals, whose *Manifesto of the Equals* declared:

> ... we can no longer endure, with the enormous majority of men, labour and sweat in the service and for the benefit of a small minority.[6]

When the Society was suppressed Babeuf and his followers began to plan an insurrection to establish a social system without rich or poor; betrayed in May 1796, Babeuf and many of his followers suffered death on the guillotine. The uprising failed, but Babeuf had initiated a conspiratorial, insurrectionary socialist tradition. This tradition was kept alive in 19th-century France by Louis-Auguste Blanqui (1805-81). Blanqui, a compulsive conspirator, spent many years in prison for his pains. Some historians have claimed that Lenin, the Russian Bolshevik leader, was also part of the conspiratorial tradition.

e) Louis Blanc

Very different from this approach was that represented by Louis Blanc (1811-82). In 1839, in *The Organisation of Work*, he recommended the state control of major industries. Blanc, as a member of the government brought to power by the 1848 revolution, established 'National Workshops' to deal with unemployment; in the event these were sabotaged by the non-socialists in the government. Despite Blanc's immediate failure, he did initiate what became known as 'reformist' socialism, that is the belief that society could move towards socialism through reforming legislation passed by existing governments. This became the political practice of the mass socialist parties of the 20th century, like the British Labour Party.

The growth of these movements, especially when set against the background of the revolutions of 1830 and 1848, made Paris a centre of socialist thought. It was, in part, these political developments that led Karl Marx to leave Germany for Paris in 1843.

4 Marx and Hegel

Germany was in the early 19th century a land of contradictions. It was economically and politically backward, divided into 36 separate states. It was also, after 1815, subject to severe political repression and censorship. On the other hand, Germany had been profoundly affected by the liberalism and nationalism of the French Revolution. These conflicting forces within German society provided the context for the arguments within Hegelian philosophy.

George Wilhelm Hegel (1770-1831) developed a philosophy that explained historical change and claimed that it had both a purpose and a motive force. He was an idealist philosopher, which means that he explained historical change in terms of interactions between ideas. The term that he used for these interactions was 'dialectic'. A dialectic is a conflict between one concept (the thesis) and another (the antithesis) that produces a third, new concept (the synthesis). In *Philosophy of History* Hegel presented the history of Western Europe as a dialectical process. The ideas of ancient Greece represented the thesis. The challenge to this society came, initially, from the criticisms of the philosopher Socrates. Over a long period of time these criticisms developed into an antithesis that stressed individual freedom. This antithesis reached its ultimate form in the French Revolution. The terror and bloodshed involved in the absolute freedom of the Revolution demonstrated the inadequacy of this antithesis and, as a consequence, a new synthesis emerged that brought together the organic stability of ancient Greece with a recognition of individual freedom. The best embodiment of this synthesis, Hegel argued, was the Prussian monarchy of the early 19th century - Hegel's own society. Hegel's dialectical conflicts took place in the realm of ideas; hence, the limited idea of freedom in Greek society was challenged by a more widely defined idea of freedom. Thus for Hegel: 'history is nothing but the progress of the consciousness of freedom because history is the development of the mind'.

This philosophy could be interpreted in two ways. It could be seen as an endorsement of the status quo given the argument that the Prussian monarchy was the synthesis at the end of the system. It seems that the Prussian authorities took this view, as they appointed Hegel professor of philosophy at the University of Berlin in 1818. The other view was that of the 'Young Hegelians'; they stressed Hegel's claim that history had motivation and movement, and argued that the Prussian monarchy was not the ultimate synthesis, but rather one stage in the unfolding historical process.

In 1836 Karl Marx (1818-1883) enrolled at the University of Berlin. Although he had enrolled to study law, he soon switched his attention to philosophy. By the end of 1837 he had read all of Hegel's works, and also joined a group of Young Hegelians. Between 1837 and 1841 this group became increasingly radical in its opinions, moving from support for constitutional monarchy to outright republicanism. Their radicalism was, however, confined to the sphere of philosophy. One of the group's leaders argued that, before intervening in the world of politics, they had to effect a revolution in humanity's ideas.

Initially Marx had thought of becoming an academic. When he graduated from Berlin in 1841 his chances of such a career were slim. Frederick William IV, who came to the throne in 1840, initiated a purge of radicals within Prussian universities. With this avenue blocked, Marx turned to journalism, becoming, in 1842, editor of the liberal paper, the *Rheinische Zeitung*. As a journalist Marx was forced to confront the practical economic and social issues that his Young Hegelian colleagues ignored. His attempts to relate his Hegelianism to such issues was the starting point for what became Marxism. According to Friedrich Engels, Marx's later collaborator:

> Marx always said it was his going into the question of the Moselle peasants that turned his attention from pure politics to economic conditions and thus to socialism.[7]

In 1843 the Prussian government suspended publication of the *Rheinische Zeitung*. Shortly after this Marx was approached by Arnold Ruge, a Young Hegelian, with a proposal that he collaborate on the production of a theoretical journal based abroad. He subsequently left for Paris to work on the *Deutsch-Franzosische Jahrbucher*.

5 Marx in Paris

In Paris Marx began to consider the gulf between Hegelian philosophy and the issues he had addressed in the *Rheinische Zeitung*. He was influenced by Ludwig Feuerbach's *Introductory Theses to the Reform of Philosophy*, published in 1843. Hegel had argued that ideas shape human existence; Feuerbach reversed this and insisted that human experience shaped ideas. In other words he replaced Hegel's idealism with materialism, that is the belief that the material world shapes human ideas. Marx rejected Hegel's belief that the government of a state was shaped by ideas. He also rejected the belief that the ideas of the state shaped the nature of society. For Hegel, a society reflected the ideas of the state, whether they be the absolute freedoms of revolutionary France or the limited freedoms conceded by the Prussian monarchy. Against this Marx argued that states reflected the needs of their society. Hence, the freedoms of revolutionary France, for him, sprang not from ideas, but from the desire of the middle classes for political, economic and social advances. He concluded that if the political state did not shape society but rather was itself shaped by society, then any criticism of the state was in reality a criticism of the social order. He further concluded that only a group with no stake in society could bring about fundamental social change. That group, Marx decided, was the proletariat, or working class. Marx thus arrived at a key element of his mature theory - that the proletariat is the agent of social change - through a philosophical route. He now had to fill in the economic details to sustain his theory.

Consequently, Marx undertook a study of British political economists. As a result of this he, like the earlier Ricardian-socialists, accepted that labour was the source of all value. Between April and August 1844 Marx set about clarifying his thoughts in a series of writings, later known as the *Economic and Philosophical Manuscripts*. Here Marx identified the existence of the class struggle, between capitalists and workers - between those who own the factories, mines, and workshops (what Marx called the means of production), and those who had nothing but the ability to work. This struggle came from the attempts of the capitalists to pay the lowest possible wage.

> For wages the lowest and only necessary rate is that required for the subsistence of the worker during work and enough extra to support a family and prevent the race of workers dying out.[8]

This situation was, in turn, the result of labour becoming a commodity, something to be bought and paid for according to the laws of supply and demand. According to Marx, the workers had to sell their labour in order to live, but the bulk of the value of what they produced went to the capitalists. Thus the wealth and power of one class increased in proportion to the decline in wealth of the proletariat.

Embedded within these developments was the phenomenon that Marx called 'alienated' labour. Within the capitalist system, he claimed, workers saw the products of their labour become merchandise in the hands of the capitalists. This meant, he argued, that workers saw the things they made as separate and distinct from themselves. As a consequence of this it was impossible to derive any sense of performing a socially beneficial act. In these circumstances workers related to production solely in terms of their ultimate financial reward.

The concept of alienation is easier to understand when related to concrete examples. In the 18th century a stocking knitter served a lengthy apprenticeship. When that was completed, it was possible for him as a skilled worker, to look forward to working at an agreed rate for items produced, a rate that would be related to the cost of living. Such a worker would produce high-quality, fully fashioned (that is, complete) garments. Like many home-based workers he determined his own hours of work, often completing the week's work in three or four very long working days, leaving the rest of the week free. Yet at the beginning of the 19th century, as the market for textile goods expanded, the merchants controlling the knitters demanded very different working conditions. They employed unapprenticed labour to drive down wage rates; they tied wages to the availability of labour, not to the cost of living; they demanded regular hours from their knitters. In some cases they required their knitters to produce knitted rectangles, which were later folded over and sewn together to produce very cheap, poor quality stockings.

As production was now tied more closely to the market for goods, so workers lost control over the work process. In many cases they were not even producing completed items. Job satisfaction in such situations suffered: one might feel proud of a well-made, complete stocking, but not of a knitted rectangle. Having no control and no pride in their work meant that workers simply became human machines, relating to their work only in terms of the wages earned. Marx argued this was alienation.

For Marx, capital represented an accumulation of past labour: that is all wealth equalled the value of all the work that had been involved in its creation. Within the capitalist system the products of labour of the whole of society become the private property of a tiny minority of that society. The private ownership of capital, and hence of the means of production, was the ultimate product of the alienation process. The conclusion to be drawn was, therefore, very simple: private property had to disappear if alienation was to be eliminated. This in turn implied the establishment of communism, described by Marx as 'the positive abolition of private property and thus of human self-alienation'.

By 1844 Marx was a materialist, as opposed to an idealist like Hegel. He had by this stage elaborated key concepts within his developing political theory: the class struggle, the structural inequalities of capitalist societies, and the need for communism as the ultimate remedy for these ills. Further elaboration and refinement of his ideas came about in collaboration with Friedrich Engels, the co-founder of modern communism.

6 Friedrich Engels

In 1841 Engels had moved to Berlin. While there he took the opportunity to attend lectures at the university and was quickly drawn into the ranks of the Young Hegelians. Engels, a keen polemicist, was soon writing pamphlets attacking Schelling, the conservative professor of philosophy. As a result he became part of the national, radical scene within Germany. In 1842 he met Moses Hess, one of Germany's self-avowed communists, and a writer for the *Rheinische Zeitung*. At this stage communism was a loosely defined doctrine which, in the case of Hess, seemed to consist of an adaptation of Saint-Simonism and a belief that commercial competition caused international conflict. Nevertheless this meeting had a great impact on Engels who from that point onwards described himself as a communist.

Later in 1842 Engels left for an extended visit to England, to work at the family-owned cotton mill of Ermen and Engels in Manchester. The trip provided him with an opportunity to observe the first modern working class, and the first working-class mass movement, Chartism. Engels recorded his observations in *The Conditions of the Working Class in England*, published in Germany in 1845. Here he drew a number of important conclusions; for example, he claimed that British society was irrevocably divided along class lines and that the resulting class conflict could not be resolved peacefully. Engels was moving towards the same political conclusions as Karl Marx, with the difference that his were rooted in first-hand experience of modern industrial conditions.

In 1844 Engels had an article published in the *Deutsch-Franzosische Jahrbucher*, the journal edited by Marx. The article came to the conclusion that the works of political economists like James Mill, David Ricardo and Adam Smith represented nothing more than a rationalisation of private property and personal greed. For Engels, the self-interest at the heart of the work of these political economists, and the removal of all restrictions on trade practices that they advocated, ensured that commerce was nothing more than 'legalised fraud'. The article greatly impressed Marx. He later gave Engels a very warm reception when he met him in August 1844. Marx and Engels had ten days of discussion during which they discovered a great deal of common ground. At the end of this period Engels returned to Germany, having established a partnership that would last until Marx's death in 1883.

7 The *Communist Manifesto*

Marx's time in Paris proved to be a very mixed experience. The journal that he had come to edit closed after one issue. Despite this Marx had been able to meet leading French socialists, such as Louis Blanc and Proudhon, and had made important advances in the development of his political theory. In 1845 the Prussian government protested to the French authorities about an issue of *Vorwarts*, containing an article by Marx that applauded an assassination attempt against the Prussian king. Marx left for Brussels.

While in Brussels, in collaboration with Engels, Marx wrote *The German Ideology*. This contains the first outline of the concept of historical materialism, a central plank of mature Marxism. This argued that the nature of society was shaped by the nature of its means of production. So, for example, in the feudal societies of the middle ages, the ownership of land was the principal basis of wealth, and consequently social status was determined by where an individual stood in terms of land ownership. At the head of society stood the king, who owned all the land in the realm; and below him were the great nobles, who were granted holdings of land in return for military service. At the bottom of society was the unfree villein, bound to a particular estate and, in effect, the property of his lord. Thus the social relations of feudal society were the product of the means of production of that society. Similarly, feudal culture, with its tales of courtly love and chivalry, sprang from the relations of production: there would have been no time for courtly love without the agricultural labour of the villeins. Marx and Engels expressed this idea thus:

1 The mode of production must not be viewed simply as reproduction of the physical existence of individuals. Rather it is the definite form of their activity, a definite way of expressing their life, a definite mode of life. What they are, therefore, coincides with what they produce. The
5 nature of individuals thus depends on the material conditions which determine their production.[9]

According to this theory, society only experiences fundamental change as a consequence of fundamental economic change. Also, all the features of a society - culture, the law, politics, etc. - ultimately reflect the way its economy is organised. This relationship is sometimes described in terms of 'base' and 'superstructure', where the economy is the base of society and all other features of that society are dependent structures resting on it. According to Engels:

1 As the state arose from the need to hold class antagonism in check ... it is, as a rule, the state of the most powerful economically dominant class. Which through the medium of the state, becomes also the politically dominant class, and thus acquires new means of holding down and
5 exploiting the oppressed class.[10]

In effect he is claiming that all the institutions of government - the State - operate in the interests of the economically dominant class.

Eventually Marx turned to practical political work. Through a correspondence committee, contact was made with a small group of working-class German exiles, in an organisation called the League of the Just. The League was made up of what Marx called 'primitive communists', who morally condemned capitalism and dreamed of replacing it with a levelled-down society. The League members based in London, however, had close connections with the Chartists and, therefore, knowledge of the world's first modern working class. This experience made them more susceptible to Marx's 'scientific communism', as it provided a coherent explanation of British social and economic developments.

In 1847 Marx and Engels were invited to join the League, and they both accepted. At the 1847 congress of the League a number of changes were made to its constitution, changes which indicate the growing influence of Marx and Engels. The name, for example, was changed to the Communist League. The League became, in effect, the first Marxist organisation. Having abandoned their old-style conspiratorial politics, the newly reorganised League required a public 'profession of faith'. Various drafts were prepared and rejected, and eventually it was decided to place this task in the hands of Marx and Engels. This was the genesis of the *Communist Manifesto*, which appeared in the early spring of 1848.

The immediate impact of the *Communist Manifesto*, even given the fact that it appeared in the year of revolutions, was slight. Its longer-term effect was to be enormous. The *Manifesto* was firmly based on a belief in the class struggle. The opening sentence states: 'The history of all hitherto existing societies is the history of class struggle.' Class conflict provided the motor for social and economic change because, it was claimed, out of class conflict ultimately sprang new societies. This was why Marx claimed that when the *bourgeoisie* created modern industry they also created the agents of their destruction, in the form of the proletariat.

The outline of class conflict that Marx and Engels provided also represented a materialist version of the Hegelian dialectic. For Hegel, history moved as a result of the clash of conflicting ideas; for Marx and Engels, social classes provided the thesis and antithesis of historical development. Hence, they argued that the landed classes of feudal society were increasingly challenged and eventually overthrown by the commercial classes (the *bourgeoisie*). The victory of the *bourgeoisie* provided the political/legal climate that made possible the development of capitalism.

The concept of alienation played a central role in the argument of the *Manifesto*. According to Marx, capital was the product of labour appropriated by the capitalist and turned into private property. This meant that the great mass of the population was denied access to the social benefits made possible through their work. The answer to this exploitative situation was communism, and the abolition of private property. This communism, as the concluding sentence indicates, was to be an international system that extended beyond national boundaries: 'WORKING MEN OF ALL COUNTRIES, UNITE !'

The *Manifesto* contained more than the ideas outlined above, but they represent the most significant parts of it. What the *Manifesto* demonstrates is that by 1848 Marxism was a developed and coherent political philosophy - even if much detailed work still remained for Marx and Engels to complete.

8 *Capital*

After the failure of the 1848 revolutions Marx spent the rest of his life as a political exile in Britain. During that time he developed and refined the economic side of his political theory in the four volumes of *Capital*. Marx argued that capitalism differed from all other previous economic systems because it was geared to the production of goods (what he called commodities) for sale, rather than goods for immediate use. In feudal societies, for example, most items produced were used by those who produced them. Under capitalism, he claimed, most goods were produced for sale on the open market.

Marx further argued that capitalists were constantly driven to expand production to increase their wealth. Industrial expansion intensified competition between capitalists and this led them to adopt measures to maintain profit margins. Mechanisation was one such measure. Another response was the division of labour. This meant that instead of making complete items, workers spent their time performing a limited number of tasks as part of the productive process.

Such methods, according to Marx, increased the rate at which *surplus value* was extracted from the working population. By this he meant that workers were only paid a fraction of the value of the goods they produced: the difference between their wage rates and the value of the goods they made was surplus value. He further claimed that surplus value was the source of all capitalist profits. An essential consequence of this was that successful attempts to increase profits meant the progressive impoverishment of the working class. Thus, capitalism was inherently exploitative and divided by a fundamental conflict between industrial workers and industrial proprietors.

Marx argued that capitalism suffered from certain in-built weaknesses that would eventually lead to its downfall. The drive to expand production meant that it was inclined to suffer from regular crises of over-production, when markets could no longer absorb the available manufactured goods. Such slumps were characterised by large-scale unemployment, which persisted until the existing market recovered and/or new ones were found. Capitalism was, therefore, according to Marx, an economic system that regularly inflicted the hardship of unemployment on the industrial population.

Superimposed on these periodic slumps was, he claimed, a long-term tendency for the rate of profit to decline. Marx arrived at this conclusion from his identification of profits with the extraction of surplus value. Industrial capitalism had a long-term tendency to mechanise to improve its competitive abilities; however, as surplus value, or profits, could only be derived from human labour, such an inclination led to a decline in the rate of profits. This, in turn, led the capitalist class to attempt to increase the rate of exploitation of the workers.

1   Except in the periods of prosperity, there rages between the capitalists the most furious combat for the share of each in the markets. This share is directly proportional to the cheapness of the product. Besides the rivalry that this struggle begets in the application of improved machinery

5   for replacing labour-power, and of new methods of production, there also

comes a time in every industrial cycle when a forcible reduction of wages beneath the value of labour-power is attempted for the purpose of cheapening commodities.[11]

Capitalism also contained, according to Marx, a fundamental contradiction. The enormous increases in productivity that it brought meant that, for the first time in history, societies had the capacity to produce plenty of material goods for all of their citizens. However, under capitalism society's productive forces operated principally for the benefit of a tiny minority. There was, in Marx's term, a conflict between the potential productivity of the *means of production*, the industrial economy, and the *relations of production*, or the system of ownership. Private control of the economy and the competition that it entailed produced the regular cycle of crises outlined above. Out of the experiences of such crises would emerge a working class that would overthrow capitalism and the rule of the *bourgeoisie*. Once freed from the constraints of competition, and operating for the benefit of society as a whole, the newly socialised economy would produce goods that were needed, rather than simply to make a profit. Within Marx's analysis the economic development of capitalism provided the material base for socialism, and the proletariat was the agent that initiated its construction.

1 Along with the constantly diminishing number of the magnates of capital, who usurp and monopolise all the advantages of this process of transformation, grows the mass of misery, oppression, slavery, degradation, exploitation; but with it too grows the revolt of the working class,
5 a class always increasing in numbers, and disciplined, united, organised by the very mechanism of the process of capitalist production itself. The monopoly of capital becomes a fetter upon the mode of production, which has sprung up and flourished along with, and under it. Centralisation of the means of production and socialisation of labour at
10 last reach a point where they become incompatible with their capitalist integument [skin]. This integument is burst asunder. The expropriators are expropriated.[12]

The proletarian revolution that Marx saw developing out of the very structure of capitalist society would, he claimed, initiate the development of communism. Trying to avoid what he saw as the errors of the utopian socialists, he wrote very little about the nature of this new society. However, it is possible to discover some of its features from comments scattered through his writings. He claimed, for example, that the removal of competition would mean the end of the division of labour. Within communist society all forms of work would be regarded as expressions of the individual's creativity, not a burden, as in capitalist society. The basis for this new society would be a situation of plenty within which people would be given what they needed, rather than just what they could afford.

The main political change within this projected communist society was the disappearance of the state. Both Marx and Engels believed that the principal role of the state was the maintenance of the status quo; hence, they argued, any challenge to the inequalities of capitalism would ultimately be met with force. In a post-revolutionary situation, however, where classes had effectively been abolished and the produce of society was shared fairly among its members, a state of the old kind would be less and less necessary. According to Engels, in such a situation:

> The state is not 'abolished'. *It withers away*[13]

By 1867, when the first volume of *Capital* was published, Marx and Engels had created a coherent doctrine that was at once a system of philosophy, an account of the processes of history, an analysis of 19th-century capitalism, and a political programme. They also believed that they had scientifically demonstrated the case for communism. Yet they said relatively little about how the transition to communism was to brought about, a problem they left to later generations of Marxists. The solutions advanced will be considered in the next chapter.

9 Conclusion

Much of this chapter has been given over to outlining the development of Marxism. This is because Marxism was a much more rigorous and complete doctrine than the other forms of socialism that emerged in the 19th century. It is also the case that the history of much of the 20th century has been dominated by self-professed Marxists, such as Joseph Stalin, Mao Zedong and Fidel Castro. Such people have even, negatively at least, determined the foreign policies of their opponents. In the 20th century, for example, the foreign policy of the United States has largely been concerned with the containment of communism.

Yet it should not be assumed that Marxism caused the immediate disappearance of other forms of socialism. In France, for example, Proudhonism remained an active movement until the end of the 19th century. In Russia political terrorism had a much higher profile than Marxism until at least the 1880s. In England socialism was a relatively weak tradition; when it did grow in the late 19th century, it owed as much to the Christianity of British nonconformity as it did to Marxism. Lenin and Trotsky, early 20th-century Russian political exiles, were highly amused to discover in Britain Labour Churches, institutions that sought to combine socialism and Christianity. Marxism was a powerful doctrine, but it still had to contend with the effects of different national traditions, an issue that will be considered in the next chapter.

Marx and Engels both regarded their approach as scientific and, indeed, their followers sometimes refer to Marxism as 'scientific socialism'. In what sense is it scientific? The four volumes of *Capital* are based on masses of material, much of it gleaned from British government publications. It might therefore be possible to accept that this analysis of 19th-century society was based on a scientific approach. However, particularly with hindsight, many of Marx's projections now seem questionable. For example, has capitalism led to the progressive impoverishment of the working class? Clearly not, in an absolute sense, at least; even those on the bottom of the social scale in Western Europe enjoy a much better standard of living than those in the same position earlier this century. Was he right about the development of revolutionary attitudes amongst the working class? The evidence would again seem to suggest not. Are modern societies split into two antagonistic social classes? The British example seems to suggest the contrary. The increase in home ownership and the growth of the white-collar sector at the expense of manual labour have both tended to increase the number of people who see themselves as middle class and who, generally, identify with the status quo. And how would Marxists explain the continuing strength of national, as opposed to class, loyalties? In Eastern Europe decades of communist rule failed to eradicate nationalistic attitudes. Do highly mechanised industries make no profit, because they have relatively few human workers? The success of the Japanese car industry would seem to prove otherwise.

All these issues suggest points at which Marxism has failed. It also seems likely that Marx was also something of a utopian. Under communism, he claimed, it would be possible to:

> ... hunt in the morning, fish in the afternoon, breed cattle after dinner, just as I like, without ever becoming a hunter, a fisherman, a herdsman, or a critic.[14]

It is difficult to imagine a modern industrial society where individuals could move so freely and randomly between occupations. It is also significant that all the occupations that Marx lists are non-industrial.

Marx's problem was that his projections were based on 19th-century capitalism. After his death social, economic, and technical developments occurred that he could not have foreseen. The emergence of state welfare schemes, and the appearance of 'consumerism', where the mass of the population, including the working class, becomes the market for industries producing personal and domestic items, to take two examples, were developments not apparent in the 19th century.

Having dealt with Marx's failures it is also worth noting that in every generation, since the 1840s, down to the present day, there have been movements claiming to be inspired by Marx. Such movements vary from huge organisations like the Chinese Communist Party to small groups like the British-based Socialist Workers' Party; they can be found in the Third World and in modern industrialised states. The influence of Marxism has varied over the decades, but it has never, so far, disappeared. However modified, it would seem that it continues to provide an explanation, for some people, for their situation and, in particular, their conflicts. There is no other theory of human conflict that has had anything like the same impact.

References
1 Leo Huberman, *Man's Worldly Goods* (Victor Gollancz, 1937), p. 197.
2 Ibid., p. 193.
3 Pat Hollis (ed.) *Class and Conflict in Nineteenth-Century England 1815-1850* (RKP, 1973), pp. 40-41.
4 J.T. Murphy, *Preparing for Power* (Pluto Press, 1972), p. 37.
5 Huberman, *Man's Worldly Goods*, p. 231.
6 Edmund Wilson, *To the Finland Station* (Penguin, 1991), p. 85
7 Boris Nicolaievsky and Otto Maenchen-Helfen, *Karl Marx: Man and Fighter* (Penguin, 1976), p. 58.
8 Karl Marx, 'Economic and Philosophical Manuscripts of 1844' in Lucio Colletti (ed.) *Early Writings. Marx* (Pelican, 1974), p. 235.
9 David McLellan, *The Thought of Karl Marx* (Papermac, 1994), p. 37.
10 F. Engels, *Origins of the Family, Private Property and the State* (Pathfinder Press, New York, 1972), p. 160.
11 Karl Marx, *Capital Vol.1* (Progress Publishers, Moscow, 1970), p. 427.
12 Ibid., p. 715.
13 V.I. Lenin, 'The State and Revolution' in *Lenin Selected Works Vol.2* (Progress Publishers, Moscow, 1970), p. 298.
14 Peter Singer, *Marx* (OUP, 1980), p. 60.

Source-based questions on 'The Development of Socialist Theory 1800-1867'

1   Five extracts from socialist theorists
Read the extracts on pages 16, 18 and 27 (Engels), and also on pages 30 and 32. Answer the following questions.
a) Explain how Hodgskin saw the role of the 'capitalist' (p. 16). (3 marks)
b) What similarities are there between Hodgskin's ideas and those of Marx (p. 30)? (6 marks)
c) What is the relationship between Owen's view of the state and Engels' (pp. 18 and 27)? (6 marks)
d) Assess the strengths and weaknesses of the interpretation advanced by Engels in this extract (p. 27). (6 marks)
e) What does this extract tell us about Marx's vision of future Communist societies (p. 32)? (4 marks)

Hints and Advice
Answering source-base questions usually involves three elements that can be summarised as: Content, Context, Significance. The first requirement is, then, that you clearly understand the meaning of the

passage. Secondly, you must be able to relate the passage to developments taking place at the time when it was written. Thirdly, what, if anything, makes the passage particularly important? In the case of these extracts the question will inevitably be: what part did they play in the development of socialist thinking? When considering socialist extracts, particularly Marxist material, a fourth element might usefully be added: language. It is very important that you have some understanding of the distinctive use of language made by 19th-century socialists, particularly Marx. You must also be careful actually to answer the question. This sound like an obvious point, but all too frequently students react to 'trigger' words like, for example, Marx, and simply write all they know about him, regardless of its relevance.

a) The danger with this question is that students might be tempted simply to paraphrase Hodgskin. As an historical exercise that would be of little value. What is required here is an explanation of Hodgskin's interpretation of the role of capitalists within early 19th-century society. Contextual knowledge is absolutely vital here. Once the literal meaning of the passage is clear, the next step is to relate it to your contextual knowledge of the socialist outlook, particularly on economics, of the period. This approach should provide a clear view of the interpretation that is being put forward.

b) In a question of this nature it is important to identify what is being compared. Hodgskin is talking about the role of the capitalist, and so the question requires you to determine what Marx is saying about the role of capitalists. It may well be that Marx is not referring to exactly the same issue that Hodgskin is addressing. What has to be considered is the question of similarities of interpretation. In other words, does Marx see the role of capitalists as broadly similar to the view advanced by Hodgskin?

c) This question asks about the *relationship* between these extracts. This means that, after determining what issues they both address, it is necessary to consider both similarities and differences. Contextual knowledge is very important here because knowledge of the respective authors' viewpoints will make it possible to give a much fuller account of their 'relationship'. The question also requires an explanation of where the two extracts stand in relation to the development of socialist thought. The question demands, in other words, some comment on the relative significance of the two passages.

d) The first step in answering this question is to decide what the key elements of the interpretation are. Having identified these the best way to criticise them is to relate them to subsequent events to determine the degree to which they have or have not proved correct. Should there be a disparity between the claims made and future developments, it would also be useful to explain that disparity by relating the extract to conditions existing at the time of writing.

e) If, as seems likely in this case, the extract does not tell you very much in terms of concrete detail, then you should consider what incidental information it carries, for example, about the essentially rural quality that it has. Does this mean that Marx's vision of communism was really a return to a pre-industrial past? Does this lack of clarity undermine his claim to be scientific in his approach? Does it suggest that he spent little time considering the nature of communist society? Why might this be the case? Finally, it would be useful to briefly compare this vision with the reality of actual communist societies.

Answering Essay Questions on 'The Development of Socialist Theory 1800-1867'

1. What were the main factors which helped the emergence of socialism in the early 19th century?
2. What were the essential features of Robert Owen's socialism?
3. Outline Marx's theory of revolution.

Hints and Advice

The key to answering essay questions is to be clear what is actually required. This often involves interpreting the question in your introduction. The main body of your work will then consist of a step-by-step progression to a conclusion, which must include a summary of your answer to the question.

Question 1. The first requirement of this question is a definition of socialism. It is also important to note that the question does not specify a country, but implies in its use of the word 'socialism' a broad movement covering more than one country. You should not therefore confine your remarks to one country. It is appropriate to suggest that some factors were more significant than others. You should also indicate that the factors varied in importance in different localities. Overall, though, you are looking to identify those factors that contributed to the emergence of socialism as an international movement. Try to avoid assertions. Always support your points with references or arguments.

Question 2. This question is asking you to break down Owen's socialism into its component parts. In your plan you can identify these with simple headings, e.g. 'justification', 'how brought about', and so on. You could also introduce an element of comparison with other forms of socialism, to demonstrate the defining features of Owen's socialism

Question 3. Firstly, you have to explain how Marx defined a revolution. Then you can break down his theory into component parts, e.g. what part do revolutions play, according to Marx, in historical development; why, according to Marx, are revolutions inevitable? In your conclusion you need to indicate the importance of revolutions for Marx's political theory in general.

Summary Diagram

The Development of Socialist Theory 1800-1867

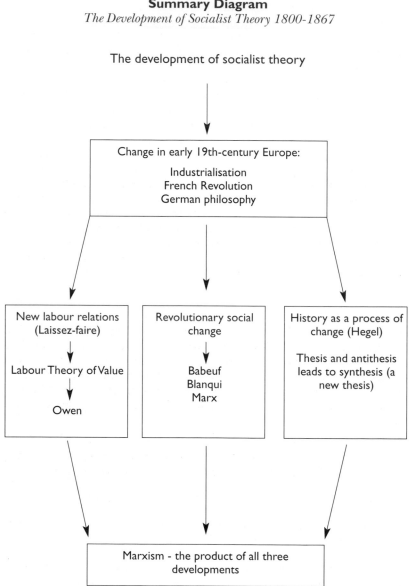

The development of socialist theory

Change in early 19th-century Europe:

Industrialisation
French Revolution
German philosophy

New labour relations (Laissez-faire)	Revolutionary social change	History as a process of change (Hegel)
Labour Theory of Value	Babeuf	Thesis and antithesis leads to synthesis (a new thesis)
Owen	Blanqui	
	Marx	

Marxism - the product of all three developments

3 Socialism Before 1914

1 Introduction

Socialists have always stressed their internationalism. In the 19th century two international organisations, the First and Second Internationals, played a major role in the growth of European socialism. At the same time, however, all European socialist parties were very much shaped by their national traditions and experiences. The central theme of this chapter is the tension between internationalism and nationalism within the socialist movement. Immediately prior to 1914, the Second International had passed resolution after resolution stressing its opposition to war. Yet when war broke out the vast majority of Europe's socialists threw themselves behind the war efforts of their national governments. The chapter will examine the development of socialism in four major European states: Germany, France, Britain and Russia. It will conclude with a section discussing the impact of the outbreak of war on European socialism as a whole.

2 Germany

The work of the First International, formed in 1864, really falls outside the scope of this chapter. However, out of the bitter conflicts that finally destroyed the International in 1876 emerged a clearer conception of the nature of a socialist party and how it should operate. This was principally the work of Karl Marx, who played a large part in the work of the International. In 1871 he drew up the following resolution for an International congress:

> 1   The working class cannot act, as a class, except by constituting itself into
> a political party, distinct from, and opposed to, all old parties formed by
> the propertied classes ... The constitution of the working class into a
> political party is indispensable in order to ensure the triumph of the
> 5   social revolution and its ultimate end - the abolition of classes.[1]

Statements of this kind, propagated through the International, were to have a profound impact on the formation of the first modern European socialist party - in Germany.

In 1863 Ferdinand Lasalle formed the General Association of German Workers (ADAV). By 1865 it had a membership of 9,500. Despite this modest progress Lasalle had successfully established an independent socialist party. That much was in line with the model laid down by Marx, but Lasalle's stress on electoral politics and state collaboration, establishing a tradition of reformism at the start of modern German socialism, clearly went against Marx's views.

Politics in Germany were complicated by the national question. The German middle classes had failed to unify Germany in the revolution of

1848. By the 1860s it seemed likely that Prussian military power would bring about German unification. Prussia, an authoritarian state, largely governed by the aristocracy, was viewed with some hostility by the liberal middle classes. Lasalle attempted to take advantage of this situation by offering the Prussian Prime Minister, Bismarck, the support of the working class, if he would give them the right to vote. Lasalle also wanted state funding for co-operative enterprises. These approaches came to nothing, but the ADAV continued to support the expansionist policies of the Prussian government, even after Lasalle's death in 1864.

The ADAV did not include all German socialists within its ranks. In southern Germany Wilhelm Liebknecht and August Bebel worked within the Union of German Workers' Societies. Politically they lined up with the middle-class People's Party of south Germany. Liebknecht and his friends, unlike the ADAV, tended to be hostile towards Prussian expansionism. In the event, circumstances conspired to push Germany's socialists together. Liebknecht's work with the People's Party was always limited by the refusal of its middle-class leadership to accept socialism. In 1866 Prussia militarily defeated Austria, and thereby knocked out the only other serious contender for dominance within Germany. With Prussia's leading role so clearly established, the national question ceased to be an issue worth arguing about. In the aftermath of this victory Bismarck created the North German Confederation which, although ruled by the monarch, had a Reichstag (parliament) based on universal manhood suffrage. This new opportunity for electoral politics provided another good reason for socialist unity. These electoral rights were extended to the whole of Germany in 1871, when the country's final unification took place.

In 1875 the rump of the ADAV amalgamated with the Social Democratic Workers' Party to form the Social Democratic Party of Germany (SPD). This was a very significant development, because the SPD was destined to become the most successful pre-First World War socialist party in Europe, if not the world. It provided other parties with organisational and ideological guidance, and came by the 1890s to be seen as the model of Marxist orthodoxy. In the light of these developments it is interesting to note that the young SPD had relatively modest beginnings. The Gotha Programme (named after the town where the founding conference was held), stated: 'The working class must initially work for its emancipation within the framework of the present-day national state'. Marx was furious at this apparent rejection of internationalism. He was also unhappy about the failure of the Gotha Programme to mention the ultimate goal of social revolution.

Exiled in London, Marx continued to exercise considerable influence on his native Germany. However, it would seem that the reformist and nationalist views of Lasalle continued to have a greater impact on German socialism. Reformism was the doctrine that social reforms could be secured in a piecemeal fashion from the existing state. Against this, Marx argued for the complete overthrow of capitalist states, before any progress could be made towards socialism.

Six years after German unification in 1871, the SPD was well on the way to becoming a major political force. In the general election of 1877 the Party won 12 seats in the Reichstag. The SPD continued to grow right up until the outbreak of the First World War. By 1912 the Party held 110 seats in the Reichstag and commanded 4.25 million votes. The principal impetus for this growth was the rapid industrialisation and urbanisation that Germany experienced in this period; between 1882 and 1907 the numbers employed in industry and manufacturing increased from over 6 million to over 11 million. By 1914 the Party drew 90 per cent of its membership from manual industrial workers.

The success of the SPD took place in an extremely hostile situation. The German State, under Bismarck, attempted, using the pretext of two assassination attempts against the Kaiser, to destroy the Party by banning it. The Anti-Socialist Law, first enacted in 1878, remained in force until 1890. The political constitution also operated to the disadvantage of radical parties, like the Social Democrats. The Imperial Parliament, based upon a franchise of all males over 25, appeared to be democratic; however, the German Chancellor and his ministers were not responsible to it, but to the Kaiser, who appointed them and dismissed them as he pleased.

These factors had the effect of radicalising the SPD. The possibility of reforms enacted through the Imperial Parliament seemed out of the question. The state was openly discriminatory, placing a disproportionate tax burden on the working class and attempting to destroy the political party to which a very large number of them gave their support. All of this seemed to confirm the Marxist view of the class nature of political states. Consequently, in 1891 the Party adopted a new programme at its congress in Erfurt. This stressed the inevitability of class conflict and economic crises and demanded the socialisation of the means of production as the only solution to the exploitation of the working class. From 1891 revolution was on the SPD's historical agenda, even if the Party remained vague about how far off it was and what could be done to hasten it.

Yet the adoption of the Erfurt Programme did not resolve the SPD's problems. Like many socialists before them, they did not satisfactorily answer the question of how to move from the capitalist present to the socialist future. In 1899 Eduard Bernstein, a leading Social Democrat, published *Evolutionary Socialism*; here he argued that the Party should abandon the ultimate goal of revolution as embodied in the Marxist Erfurt Programme, and recognise the reality that the SPD was essentially a reformist party. Bernstein based his arguments on the observation that class divisions in Germany were not sharpening, and that living standards were generally rising. He may also have been influenced by the social reforms - like social insurance - introduced by Bismarck in the 1880s, as these seemed to demonstrate that it was possible to gain meaningful concessions from the German State. Taken together, these propositions also denied that capitalism was prone to ever worsening crises and compelled constantly to drive down the living standards of the working class. Whatever the merits of Bernstein's 'revisionist' views, they failed to explain how reforms could be secured by the SPD, given the fact that German governments were at liberty to ignore the views of the Imperial Parliament.

It was precisely this point that was made in the attacks launched on Bernstein at the 1899 and 1903 party congresses. The argument clearly struck a chord with the Party membership, as Bernstein was routed at both congresses. In a speech attacking Bernstein, a leading Social Democrat made the following point:

> What Darwin has discovered in the history of nature, what he has asserted concerning the laws of biological process, has been applied by Marx to human society and its progress. Marx, in fact has discovered the laws of social development.[2]

The defeat of Bernstein had not answered the question of how to move towards the ultimate socialist goal. The comparison of Marx to Darwin suggested that the movement towards socialism was part of a 'natural' process of social development and was, therefore, something that would happen of its own accord. In retrospect, it is possible to see that this failure to deal with this key question would cause the SPD problems in the future; at the time it seemed as if Marxist orthodoxy had prevailed within the Party. Having apparently settled the issue of 'revisionism' in Germany, the Party set itself the task of imposing orthodoxy on the whole of the Socialist International.

Karl Kautsky, editor of the Party's theoretical journal, played a key part in defeating Bernstein, and in promoting Marxist orthodoxy within the International. On the face of it Kautsky's political credentials seemed beyond question. In 1898 he had written:

> But if once the materialist conception of history as the motive force of the coming social revolution were abandoned, then I would have to admit that I was through, that my life no longer had any meaning.[3]

However, despite this apparently unequivocal attachment to revolutionary Marxism, Kautsky did not develop a concrete strategy for advancing the socialist revolution. He disagreed with the ideas of Bernstein, but did not, or could not, develop an alternative form of political action. Kautsky's role within the Party becomes clearer if we look at the course taken by one of the Party's left-wing minority, Rosa Luxemburg. In 1899, in *Social Reform or Revolution*, she wrote:

> Legal reform and revolution are not different methods of historical progress that can be picked out at pleasure from the counter of history ... They are different moments in the development of class society which condition and complement each other ...[4]

This was a view that all sections of the Party could agree with, provided it was accepted that they were currently within the 'moment' of legal reform. Kautsky's and Luxemburg's defence of Marxism in this period unified the Party because it did not necessarily involve any attempt to move from theory to practice.

In the years leading up to 1914 the SPD continued along an increasingly reformist path. The combined influence of the trade unions and the growing party bureaucracy worked to place legal reformism at the forefront of the Party's activity. These sections of the Party saw electoral activity as central to the Party's success. From this identification with election to state bodies, the Party moved to identify with the state itself. If election to such bodies represented the entire reason for the Party's whole existence, any threat to those bodies was also a threat to the Party.

Kautsky continued to use revolutionary language and follow a reformist practice. Luxemburg, on the other hand, very much influenced by the 1905 Russian Revolution, developed a position that placed great emphasis on the use of the general strike as a political weapon. This move reflected her disillusionment with the parliamentary reformism of the leadership.

On the eve of the First World War, then, beneath the apparent ideological certainty and organisational strength of the SPD, a number of forces were at work. The largely ritualistic adherence to Marxism, combined with the very real identification with the organisations of the German State, explains the overwhelming support given by the SPD for the declaration of war. They genuinely believed that they had to defend their state from the Russians and the French. At the same time, the very wide range of positions held by SPD members meant that its long-term chances of continuing unity were small. Up to 1914 the SPD had contained the widest range of socialist positions, united by a formal, but empty, commitment to Marxism. The compromise immediately collapsed at the outbreak of war when it was necessary either to become an outright supporter or an outright opponent of the German State.

3 French Socialism

Shortly before his death in 1883 Marx, observing the difficulties of French Marxists, remarked to Engels: 'one thing is certain I am not a Marxist!' These difficulties were vividly illustrated by the circumstances of the founding of the Second, or Socialist International, in 1889. In the years following the collapse of the First International, rapid industrialisation, and the example of German Social Democracy, encouraged the formation of socialist parties throughout Europe. This development generated a call for a new International. The emotional appeal of creating such a body in Paris, in the centenary year of the storming of the Bastille, proved overwhelming, and

so the French socialists were asked to organise a founding conference. In the event, so divided were they that two separate conferences
were organised. The one organised by the Marxist, French Workers'
Party (POF) is generally accepted as the starting point for the
International. It is, however, ironic that despite achieving international unity, divisions between French socialists remained as sharp as
ever. These divisions centred on the old problem of how actually to
achieve socialism, but they were given a particular character by
French circumstances.

Industrialisation in France occurred later and at a slower rate than
in Britain and Germany. As late as 1896, 36 per cent of French workers
were employed in establishments with five or fewer employees. On the
brink of the First World War, over 40 per cent of the working population was employed in agriculture. French socialists did not, as in
Germany, have masses of newly urbanised workers employed in
massive industrial plants; instead they had to deal with a nation whose
slow rate of change allowed the survival of older attitudes, including
early forms of socialism, like Proudhonism (see pages 20-21).

Recent French history had produced a variety of contradictory attitudes on the French left. The experience of repression between 1830
and 1870 made many deeply suspicious of the state and of *bourgeois*
parties. The POF resolutely opposed the idea that there was a
reformist road to socialism and vigorously opposed co-operation with
non-socialist parties. Against this view were those socialists who saw
the democratic institutions of the Third Republic, established in
1871, as both progressive and usable. These socialists pressed for
reforms that were immediately possible, and consequently became
known as 'possibilists'. This reformist approach was also promoted by
a group of French parliamentarians, who became known as the
Independent socialists. One member of this group, Alexandre
Millerand, caused an international furore in socialist circles, when he
accepted a cabinet post in the *bourgeois* government formed in 1898.

A third strategy was developed by the trade unions. Trade unionism
was weak in France: at the beginning of the 20th century only 10 per
cent of French workers were organised into unions. French employers
also proved very reluctant to recognise unions and negotiate with
them. This lack of recognition, combined with a disenchantment with
parliamentary politics, led the CGT (the General Confederation of
Workers), the principal French trade union federation, to adopt
syndicalism. This was the doctrine that society could be transformed
by industrial action. Syndicalists argued that the trade union should
not principally concern itself with issues of pay and conditions but
should become 'a fighting organisation [which] will in the future be
an organisation for production and distribution and the basis of
social reorganisation'.[5] However, up until 1914 the CGT only had
400,000 members, out of an industrial workforce of six million, and
was therefore unable to effect its long-term programme.

By 1890 the principal factions of French socialism had formed two political parties, the reformist French Socialist Party (PSF) and the Marxist Socialist Party of France (PS de F). This division proved disastrous. Both parties contested elections, often in the same constituencies. In one 1902 contest both parties received a joint share of 18 per cent of the vote in a constituency where, in 1898, one socialist party had polled 32 per cent. Electoral problems, the issues raised by the Dreyfus case (Dreyfus was a Jewish-French army officer falsely imprisoned for treason), and the entry of Millerand into a *bourgeois* government - all drew the French socialists to the attention of the leading German Social Democrat, Karl Kautsky.

A fear of compromising their politics by contact with *bourgeois* politicians had kept the PS de F, unlike the PSF, from involvement in the Dreyfus case. It was this independent, working-class approach that gained the PS de F the support of Kautsky against the French reformists. As the leading Marxist writer in Europe - often referred to as the 'Pope of Marxism' - and as a member of the highly successful SPD, Kautsky had enormous prestige within the International. It was, therefore, of considerable significance when he successfully proposed a resolution at the 1900 congress of the International condemning Millerand's action.

The PS de F capitalised on this support by linking its opposition to French reformism with the SPD's conflict with Bernstein's 'revisionism'. Jules Guesde, a leading member of the PS de F, introduced a resolution to the 1904 congress of the International that was entirely based on the anti-revisionist resolution passed at the 1903 SPD congress. This:

1 … condemned attempts to change our past and always victorious policy based on class struggle [and which] substituted for the conquest of political power a policy of accommodation to the existing order. The revisionist tactic would turn a party which was revolutionary into one
5 which would be content to reform the [existing] bourgeois society.[6]

Clearly this argument applied as much to French as to German 'revisionism'. This international pressure, combined with the discrediting of Millerand (he had left office in 1903, but not before supporting the use of armed troops against strikers), finally brought about the unification of French socialism, with the formation in 1905 of the SFIO (French Section of the Workers' International). The SFIO, with its Marxist programme, was closely modelled on the SPD and had many features in common with the German party. Like the Germans, the SFIO combined an adherence to an ultimate revolutionary goal with a day-to-day engagement with electoral politics. The SFIO also enjoyed a period of significant growth, so that by 1914 it achieved a vote of 1.4 million and won 103 seats in the National Assembly.

The SFIO also had a number of problems. Like the SPD the SFIO, despite its growing strength, seemed condemned never to enjoy power because of its refusal to make political alliances with non-socialists. This was a particular problem in a country where the working class did not form the majority of the population. Although the Party made some advances in the rural south, particularly in the wine-growing regions, there were still, in 1914, key industrial areas where the Party was very weak. Also, the unity of the SFIO was perhaps more apparent than real. The Party contained a broad spread of opinions, from orthodox Marxism to quasi-syndicalism. The SFIO also had a very poor relationship with the CGT trade union federation. These factors meant that the French left was much better at revolutionary rhetoric than revolutionary action. In the period before 1914 there was no prospect of either the syndicalists of the CGT or the Marxists of the SFIO coming to power.

4 British Socialism

One of the surprising features of European politics in the late 19th century was the weakness of socialism in the United Kingdom. Britain had, prior to the 1880s, a well-organised trade union movement - albeit one that catered largely for skilled workers - but its leadership was overwhelmingly Liberal in political allegiance. With the demise in the late 1840s of Chartism - a working-class movement for electoral reform that had a socialist element within it - socialism virtually disappeared in this country until the 1880s. Engels argued that this was because the English working class, sharing in the prosperity produced by Britain's industrial monopoly in 1850-1880, had adopted the politics and values of their employers.

An alternative explanation is that the relatively slow pace of industrialisation in the UK, in comparison with Germany, for example, allowed the persistence of older attitudes and values. A good example of this could be found in the South Wales coalfield, where, almost until the end of the 19th century, miners tended to see themselves *along with the mine owners*, as the progressive classes, opposing the parasitic 'feudal' land-owning classes. Such a polarisation did not reflect Marxist notions of class conflict but, rather, the radical-democratic attitudes of the 18th century.

These explanations are not mutually exclusive. They could both operate to varying degrees in different localities with different workforces. However, they do both underscore the point that socialism was late re-emerging in Britain and was extremely weak when it did appear. In Germany and France there were, by the 1880s, significant parties and trade union movements committed to creating societies in which production was controlled by the state and geared to satisfying social needs, not creating profits. In Britain the vast majority of the working class endorsed private ownership, through their support of the Liberal Party. At this point all socialists saw the public ownership of the economy as a central feature of their political creed. The belief of British trade unionists that the profits of privately owned companies benefited the nation in general, and that therefore state ownership was not necessary, placed them well outside the socialist camp.

A key question to be addressed is why did socialism reappear in Britain after such a long absence? This development appears to be the product of several interlocking factors. During the 1880s it became apparent that Britain's period of economic dominance was ending. Between 1870 and 1913 the British share of international industrial production fell from 30 per cent to 15 per cent. This relative decline was accompanied by series of depressions, which in turn produced large-scale and sometimes violent demonstrations by the unemployed. This change of fortunes sapped the faith of some, mainly amongst the middle classes, in the inevitability of progressive improvement under capitalism. A small but significant middle-class following for socialism began to develop. Extensive social surveys, such as those conducted by Charles Booth, demonstrated that poverty was the result of the way society was organised, not the moral failings of individuals. For example, Booth demonstrated that no matter how hard casually employed labourers worked, their irregular employment and low levels of income made it impossible for them to escape poverty.

This, then, was the context for the appearance of Britain's first national socialist organisation, the Democratic Federation. This was largely the result of the efforts of H.M. Hyndman, a wealthy stockbroker who had been converted to socialism by reading Marx's *Capital*. Initially the Federation's political orientation was similar to that of the working-class radicals who operated on the left wing of British Liberalism. However, by 1884, when it changed its name to the Social Democratic Federation (SDF), it had become an explicitly Marxist organisation. The Federation had some early successes in recruiting a number of very able working-class organisers. Many of these figures became prominent in the movement to unionise the unskilled in the late 1880s. The organisation also achieved some notoriety for organising the unemployed. SDF-led demonstrations frequently ended in violence; an attempt physically to break a police ban on demonstrations to Trafalgar Square led to the deaths of three demonstrators in November 1887, an event subsequently dubbed 'Bloody Sunday'.

However, despite this prominence, the SDF had a membership of only 3,259 in 1897. The SDF undoubtedly played a part in reintroducing Marxism to British politics and in training a generation of socialists who went on to gain prominence in other organisations. That said, the SDF itself failed to make a political breakthrough and did not achieve the electoral success it desired. Essentially the organisation suffered from three problems. The first of these was its attitude towards trade unions. Although many individual SDF members were actively engaged in union work, as an organisation the SDF rejected trade unionism as a diversion from the fight for socialism. Such an outlook prevented the SDF from fully taking advantage of the massive growth in trade union organisation that took place in the last 20 years of the 19th century.

The second problem was Hyndman's character. Within the SDF his manner was autocratic and authoritarian, leading one member to comment: 'Hyndman can only accept one position in such a body as the SDF - that of master'.[7] The difficulties presented by Hyndman's character intensified the arguments around the SDF's third problem, how actually to proceed to socialism. Hyndman favoured a combination of propaganda and electoral work. A majority of the SDF's council rejected such an approach and split from the main body to form the Socialist League, at the end of 1884. Their view was that socialists should conduct propaganda work until the final collapse of capitalism made it possible to take direct action to seize power. The League, despite the membership of the designer William Morris, never numbered more than a few hundred, and declined rapidly when he left in 1890.

A very different organisation was the Fabian Society, also formed in 1884. The Fabians, numbering only a few hundreds, were predominantly middle class in origin, and resolutely opposed to the Marxist notion of class war. For them socialism represented the most efficient way of running society: it was, they argued, a system that allowed the expert the opportunity fully to exercise his or her talents. It is easy to see how such a view would appeal to middle-class professionals. For much of this period they rejected the idea of a separate socialist party and sought instead to influence the thinking of existing parties. For example, they urged the London Radicals not to break with liberalism, but to stay inside the party and permeate it with socialist ideas. They believed that socialism would come gradually as more and more spheres of life came under government or municipal control; every new council bus service or gasworks was a further advance towards socialism. The Fabians were essentially an intellectual grouping promoting new ideas through publications and lectures. It was only in the 20th century that they became committed to the idea of a separate socialist party, but thereafter they exercised great influence over the Labour Party. One of their best-known members, Sidney Webb, wrote the Labour Party's 1918 constitution.

A key problem for British socialists in this period was the loyalty of large sections of the working class to the Liberal Party; this was typified by the Lib-Lab MPs (11 of them in 1885). They were MPs of working-class origin - mainly from mining constituencies - who took the Liberal whip in the Commons, but sought to raise issues of particular concern to the Labour Movement. In the 1880s industrial conflict placed considerable strain on this Liberal-Labour alliance.

During the 1887 Scottish miners' strike a local leader, Keir Hardie, was struck by the lack of support from the local Liberals. Hardie's disenchantment with the Liberals was subsequently increased by their refusal to support him as a Parliamentary candidate. Undeterred, Hardie stood as an independent miners' candidate; he lost, but his campaign led to the formation of the Scottish Labour Party in 1888. Similar developments were taking place in other areas. In Bradford the hostility of local Liberals towards striking textile workers played a large part in the creation of the Bradford Labour Union, an organisation that claimed 3,000 members by the end of 1892. In various parts of the country this period saw the formation of local independent - independent of the Liberals - labour parties. The 1892 general election saw a number of independent labour candidates, including Keir Hardie, elected to Parliament. This helped to stimulate a demand for a national Independent Labour Party (ILP). Such a party was duly formed in 1893.

On the face of it the ILP had a number of advantages. It was easily the largest British socialist party, claiming a membership of 35,000 in 1895. It also had strong links with the trade union movement, and was securely based in the north of the country, amongst Britain's principal industries. Doctrinally, however, it had weaknesses. At the founding conference delegates had rejected a proposal to put the word 'socialist' in its title, on the grounds that it might put off potential voters. This established what was to prove a long-term feature of British socialism, a tendency to adjust to existing outlooks, rather than convert people to new ones. The ILP nevertheless regarded itself as socialist. However, the Party remained vague about what socialism was. Very often the ILP is described as believing in 'Ethical Socialism'. This seems little more than the encouragement of desirable attitudes - fairness, good fellowship, etc. - within society. This approach is typified by Keir Hardie's 1892 election poster, with its demands for: 'Justice to Labour', 'Fair Rents', etc. Although commendable in itself, such an approach did not resolve issues of political strategy. In the event the ILP became a pragmatic, reforming, electoral party. The 1884 Reform Act, which had increased the electorate by two million to a total of five million, made it possible for socialist parties to adopt an electoral approach. However, it is worth noting that 40 per cent of the male population and all of the female population remained without the vote until 1918. Although it lost its one MP, Hardie, in 1895, the Party had a reasonable degree of success in local elections. By 1900 it had 106 councillors, 66 School Board members, and 51 Poor Law Guardians.

In an attempt to achieve a national political breakthrough the ILP promoted the idea of the 'Labour Alliance' between the socialist groups and the trade unions. In 1900 their efforts seemed to bear fruit with the creation of the Labour Representation Committee

(LRC). This became the Labour Party in 1906. Not all of the unions affiliated to the LRC. The miners, for example, did not join until 1910, and many of the unions that did affiliate had Liberal leaders. This meant that the socialist organisations affiliated to the LRC had to compromise over their objectives. The Social Democratic Party (the new name of the SDF) could not accept this and left the LRC. The LRC was not a socialist organisation. Its agenda was to secure legislation that would benefit Labour in the broadest sense. Trade union leaders were particularly keen to reverse a series of hostile legal judgements that threatened union practices and funds.

By 1914 the Labour Party had over 40 MPs. However, the Party's success was almost entirely the product of a secret agreement with the Liberals, whereby the parties agreed not to oppose their respective candidates. It should also be noted that many of Labour's MPs were really Liberals. This was largely true of the Miners' MPs who accepted the Labour whip when the Miners' Federation affiliated to the Party in 1910. Within the Commons Labour, to all intents and purposes, became an adjunct of the Liberal Party. The advance of Labour's Parliamentary representation did not therefore represent an advance for socialism.

The lack of success of the Parliamentary Labour Party (PLP) generated considerable criticism. There was discontent in the ILP; some disillusioned members joined the British Socialist Party (BSP),

VOTE FOR

Home Rule.

Democratic Government.

Justice to Labour

No Monopoly.

No Landlordism

Temperance Reform.

Healthy Homes.

Fair Rents.

Eight-Hour Day.

Work for the Unemployed.

KEIR HARDIE.

1892 General Election poster for Keir Hardie

formed in 1911 at the initiative of the SDP. Syndicalism, the doctrine of revolutionary change brought about by industrial action, also seemed to grow in influence. The year 1910 saw the beginning of the 'Great Labour Unrest', a series of large-scale strikes that continued up to the outbreak of war. It seems unlikely that the majority of strikers were motivated by anything other than economic needs, although syndicalists did play a part in the leadership of many strikes. What all of these developments do suggest is a fluid situation in which it was by no means certain that the Labour Party would emerge as the dominant form of British socialism.

5 Russian Socialism

Russian socialists in the late 19th century faced very different problems from their Western European comrades. The Russian State was an autocracy with political power centralised in the hands of the Tsar. A national parliament, the *Duma*, was created only in an attempt to head off the 1905 revolution. Even then Nicholas II saw it as consultative rather than legislative body. This politically backward state rested on a largely peasant-based agricultural economy. Russian socialists before 1905 had therefore no democratic institutions to work through, and a proportionally tiny industrial proletariat to mobilise. At the turn of the century Russia had 2.4 million industrial workers, but a peasant population of more than 90 million.

The first generation of Russian socialists, the *Narodniks* (from the Russian for people, *Narod*), made a virtue of these apparent weaknesses. Like the French socialist Proudhon (see pages 20-21), the *Narodniks* advocated a socialism that sought to preserve existing communities against the advance of capitalism. They argued that bodies like the peasant commune could act as the basis for a direct transition to socialism, entirely missing out the capitalist stage of development. Within the communes the distribution of farmland amongst the households was decided collectively, according to their size and requirements. This obviously involved a conception of fairness, allocating land in accordance with need rather than wealth, and it is easy to see how this could be interpreted as the basis for a kind of peasant-socialism.

In the 1870s a wave of young intellectuals, inspired by such ideas, went into the countryside to conduct political agitation amongst the peasantry. This proved to be a disillusioning experience. The young *Narodniks* were met with suspicion and hostility. A significant number of them were turned over to the police. In response to this failure, a section of the *Narodniks* turned to terrorism. It was argued that terrorist acts would break down popular reverence for Tsarist authority, and thus it was believed that a successful assassination would lead to a mass mobilisation of the people. The name of the terrorist group - the People's Will - was indicative of the role that these intellectuals took upon themselves; it implied that they knew what the people wanted, better than the people themselves. This assumption of leadership by middle-class intellectuals was to prove an enduring feature of Russian socialism. In 1881 the People's Will assassinated Tsar Alexander II. However, nothing but heavy state repression followed: the death of the Tsar did not produce a mass mobilisation of the people. The Tsar was dead but Tsarism remained.

These events led a small group of *Narodniks* to review their political outlook, and come up with a radically different political perspective. In 1883 three Russian exiles formed Russia's first Marxist organisation, the Group for the Emancipation of Labour. The most important figure in the group, Georgi Plekhanov, formulated three basic positions. Firstly, he argued that Russia was - in the 1880s - already a capitalist society. The freeing of the serfs in the 1860s, he claimed, had created the conditions for waged labour, that is, labour sold as a commodity, one of the bases of the capitalist system. From this he argued that Russia was moving rapidly towards factory production, which in turn meant the creation of an industrial proletariat; such a class would by its very nature become, at least potentially, the most revolutionary in Russia. These two positions clearly refuted the arguments of the *Narodniks*. Plekhanov's third position, however, closely reflected their views. Here he argued that the superior knowledge of the intelligentsia meant that it was they who would lead the revolution.

In the early 1880s the prospects for direct political action of the kind favoured by Plekhanov's group were slight, but within a decade, conditions in Russia were transformed. Industrialisation moved forward very rapidly in the last twenty years of the 19th century. Between 1885 and 1895 the working class doubled in size. Clearly it remained a small minority within the population as a whole, but it was highly concentrated in a limited number of centres, and often employed in massive industrial plants. The Putilov metalworks in St Petersburg, for example, had 12,000 workers, making it one of the largest factories in the world. It has been calculated that the working class produced one-third of Russia's national income. Agriculture, which employed the vast majority of the population, produced a half.

6 The Role of Lenin

These developments demolished the notion that Russia could avoid a capitalist stage. They also stimulated a growth of interest in Marxism and the formation of Marxist groups. One of these, the Union of Struggle for the Emancipation of the Working Class, based in St Petersburg, numbered Vladimir Ulianov, better known as Lenin, amongst its members. The militancy of Russian workers also encouraged the spread of Marxism; in 1896, for example, textile workers began a strike in St Petersburg that eventually involved over 30,000 people. At that point many Russian Marxists, including Lenin, believed that industrial militancy would inevitably lead to political militancy.

Within a short time Lenin was dramatically to reverse this position and argue that only the intervention of middle-class revolutionaries would move the workers from industrial militancy to revolutionary socialism. This reversal typified the problems facing Russian Marxists. In 1898 a Russian Social Democratic Labour Party was formed. This development did not, however, resolve key issues of strategy and tactics. One central question for Russian Marxists was the nature of the society that would be created by a successful revolution. It was taken for granted by Marxists that societies pass through stages in their development (see page 28). Russia, it was argued, was a feudal society and would, therefore, have to undergo a bourgeois-democratic revolution. In 1895 Lenin wrote:

> The Social-Democratic Party declares that it will support all the strata of the bourgeoisie engaged in the struggle against the autocratic government. The democratic struggle is inseparable from the socialist one.[8]

This, however, did not explain the role that Marxists would play in the revolution. What, for example, would they do once a bourgeois-democratic government had been established? Another issue that divided Russian socialists was that of the Party's relationship to the working class. One group argued that socialists should primarily support the economic demands of striking workers, in the belief that economic demands would develop into political ones. But by 1900 figures like Lenin and Plekhanov rejected this approach, and argued that political demands should be at the forefront of the Party's work. Last, but by no means least, was the issue of party organisation. The Social Democratic parties of Western Europe, operating openly and legally, provided no model for the Russians to follow. Lenin, emerging from political exile in Siberia in 1900, applied himself to solving these problems. When he placed his proposals before the Second Congress of the Russian Social Democratic Party in 1903, they produced an irrevo-cable split between the Bolsheviks (majority men), Lenin's followers, and the Mensheviks (minority men), led by Julius Martov.

The central issue in dispute was the definition of Party membership. On the face of it the differences seemed quite small. Martov's version stated that a member:

> ... accepts the Party's programme and supports the Party both financially and by regular work under the control and direction of one of the Party organisations.

Lenin's version stated that a Party member:

> ... accepts the Party's programme and supports the Party both financially and by personal participation in one of its organisations.[9]

According to Lenin, Martov's version did not imply membership of a Party organisation, and non-membership meant that the Party could only exercise a limited control over its supporters. What was at issue here was a conflict between the idea of a highly centralised and tightly disciplined party, and a much looser and more liberal form of organisation. This is confirmed by Martov's later claim that Lenin's formulation

1   ... eliminated not only numerous intellectuals who sympathised with the party and rendered it assistance while finding themselves incapable of joining an illegal organisation, but also a large part of social democratic workers who constituted a link between the Party and the masses
5   but who for reasons of expediency refused to join its ranks.[10]

The Bolsheviks and Mensheviks also disagreed over the nature of the revolution. As far back as the 1880s Plekhanov had argued that the next revolution, although bourgeois-democratic in character, would be led by the proletariat. Lenin later described the bourgeois-democratic revolution in these terms:

1   Since Russia is most backward and has not yet completed its bourgeois revolution, it still remains the task of Social-Democrats in that country to achieve three fundamental conditions for consistent democratic reform, viz. [namely], a democratic republic (with complete equality and
5   self-determination for all nations), confiscation of the landed estates, and an eight-hour working day.[11]

At the 1903 congress Lenin accused the Mensheviks of abandoning the idea of proletarian leadership of the *bourgeois* revolution, in order to develop a closer relationship with Russian Liberals. Lenin and the Bolsheviks rejected the idea that the Liberal *bourgeoisie* could play a positive role in the achievement of these objectives. They argued that the Russian *bourgeoisie* was too weak and too compromised with Tsarism genuinely to fight for a democratic revolution. This, it was claimed could only be achieved by the proletariat in alliance with the peasantry.

In hindsight it is clear that the splits at the 1903 congress created two opposing parties. It was not, however, so clear at the time. Indeed there appeared to be a reunification of the Party at the 1906 congress. In the event, the pressures of war and revolution exaggerated the divergent lines of development of these factions. What is clear is that Lenin, a party leader in his own right after 1903, was developing his own distinctive solution to the problem of the transition from capitalism to socialism. This involved a highly centralised party of professional revolutionaries operating under military-style discipline. This new style of party would profoundly alter the history of Russia, and the rest of the world.

7 Conclusion

It should be clear from this chapter that socialism was advancing in Europe and the Russian Empire at the end of the 19th century. Most of these socialist parties were Marxist in orientation. All of them were linked together through the Socialist International. Within the International the German SPD played a dominant role: the French SFIO, for example, was directly modelled on the SPD. The SPD also exercised considerable influence on Russian socialists, one of them wrote in 1914: 'It was for us not one of the parties of the International, but *the* party.'[12] The key issue that appeared to unite all sections of the International was opposition to war. Successive congresses of the International had passed major anti-war resolutions. In 1914 the 'war' policy of the International was still based on a resolution passed at the 1907 Stuttgart congress. This stated:

> 1 If war threatens to break out, it is the duty of the working class to use every effort to prevent war by all means that seem to them appropriate.
>   Should war none the less break out, their duty is to intervene to bring it promptly to an end, and to use the political and economic crisis
> 5 to rouse the masses from their slumbers and hasten the downfall of capitalist domination.[13]

When war broke out the vast majority of European socialists did not attempt to hasten the downfall of capitalism. Instead they threw their weight behind their national governments.

This abrupt about-turn obviously presents students with a major problem: how is it to be explained? As with any complex historical development no one simple explanation is completely satisfactory; similarly, none of the following explanations apply with equal force to all of the countries considered. The most obvious explanation is that the leaders of European socialism were not sincere in their anti-war pledges. This is not to say that they wanted war, rather that they had no intention of calling general strikes to stop one. Albert S. Lindemann has suggested that the real purpose of their anti-war resolutions was to satisfy (and quieten) socialists on the left-wing of the International. There is no way of conclusively proving this, but the subsequent actions of leading figures do give the idea some credence.

A second explanation argues that the mechanical Marxism of the Second International did not allow these parties to stand against major historical trends. As we have seen (see page 40), the German Social Democrat Bebel argued that society developed according to laws similar to those that Darwin had discovered in nature. The implication of this was that the Party would have to *wait* for the revolution, not *make* it. Consequently, the war was seen as a major historical development that could not be opposed by direct, revolutionary action, but had to be accepted.

Another reason for accepting the war was the intense wave of nationalist feeling that swept the combatant countries. Socialist leaders feared losing the support of their followers if they opposed the war.

> As one German social-democratic leader later put it - and the situation was identical in France - he and his comrades voted for war credits to avoid being beaten to death by their followers.[14]

The patriotic outpourings that greeted the war demonstrated the enduring appeal of nationalism within Western European society. What is perhaps more surprising are the many examples of nationalist feeling within the socialist movement. Hyndman, leader of the British SDF, had been very reluctant to join the Socialist International, for fear of foreign domination. Bebel, the German Social Democrat is recorded as saying 'If it is against Russia I myself will grab a gun.'[15] No doubt many German Social Democrats, in the summer of 1914, speculating about the effect of a general strike against the war, concluded that a German strike would be more effective than a Russian one and could, therefore, lead to a successful invasion by the forces of the Russian autocracy. Germany might only enjoy a limited democracy, but it was clearly preferable to the Russian alternative.

As well as nationalistic feeling within the socialist parties there was also a profound identification with national traditions and institutions. German Social Democrats had grown up with the unified German Empire; they were familiar with its institutions and had prospered under them. British socialists and trade unionists were steeped in the traditions of 19th-century liberalism, and identified with its support for democratic and nationalist movements in Europe. The sight of 'poor little Belgium' having its neutrality violated by Prussian militarism awakened all those old sentiments. In France Jules Guesde, former scourge of the *bourgeoisie*, became a fervent supporter of the war effort against the national enemy.

It would seem, therefore, that class loyalties - particularly international class loyalties - were unable to overcome national loyalties. It may also be the case that those parties operating within democratic states had no choice but to shape their policies to the attitudes of the electorate. Nationalism was a potent force in 19th-century Europe and affected both Socialists and their policies. It is surely significant that the only group that maintained a consistent anti-war position was the Bolshevik faction of the Russian Social Democratic Labour Party. The Bolsheviks called for the military defeat of their own government and the conversion of the war into a revolutionary class war. Russia, of course, had a very weak democratic tradition. Its government policies were ultimately the responsibility of the Tsar. Fundamental criticism of the government in Russia did not imply the election of a new one, but, logically, the replacement of the whole system.

So, at the end of August 1914, the hopes of socialist internationalism were shattered. However, although internationalism was dead, the socialist parties were not and in the inter-war period they achieved power in Germany, France and Great Britain. The Socialist International was also revived, although it was a much looser body in the post-1919 period, and never attempted to impose policies on the affiliated parties. After the war the socialist parties openly became what they had always really been, national parties, promoting a variety of national forms of socialism.

References

1   David Fernbach (ed.), *Marx. The First International and After* (Penguin, 1974), p. 48.
2   A. Ramos Oliveira, *A People's History of Germany* (Gollancz, 1942), p. 62.
3   Davis McLellan, *Marxism After Marx* (Papermac, 1980), p. 37.
4   Ibid., p. 45.
5   Walter Kendall, *The Labour Movement in Europe* (Allen Lane, 1975), p. 38.
6   W.L. Guttsman, *The German Social Democratic Party 1875-1933* (George Allen and Unwin, 1981), p. 296.
7   Yvonne Kapp, *Eleanor Marx. The Crowded Years 1884-1898* (Virago, 1979), p. 60.
8   Richard Pipes, *The Russian Revolution 1899-1919* (Harvill, 1997), p. 354.
9   McLellan, *Marxism After Marx*, p. 72.
10 Ibid.. p. 73.
11 V.I. Lenin, 'The War and Russian Social Democracy' (1914), in *Lenin Selected Works Vol.1* (Progress Publishers, Moscow, 1970), p. 656.
12 Isaac Deutscher, *The Prophet Armed. Trotsky 1879-1921* (Oxford University Press, 1963), p. 214.
13 *Everybody's Book of Politics* (Odhams Press, 1937), p. 337.
14 Albert S. Lindemann, *A History of European Socialism* (Yale University Press, 1983), p. 189.
15 Sebastian Haffner, *Failure of a Revolution. Germany 1918-19* (André Deutsch, 1973), p. 15.

Answering Essay Questions on 'Socialism before 1914'

Essay questions in this area could focus on single countries, or take a wider approach. The following examples are of both types:
1.   Account for the rise of socialism in the late 19th century.
2.   How is it possible to explain the SPD's espousal of Marxism and its commitment to electoral politics?
3.   Why did the International fail to oppose the outbreak of the First World War?
4.   What was the significance of the 1903 split in the Russian Social Democratic Labour Party?

Every decent essay must have a beginning, a middle and an end. In the study guides in this book, advice will be given on each stage. First, the opening paragraph. Here you should aim to do several things: i) explain the meaning of the question, defining key terms and establishing the parameters of the question; ii) break the question into several smaller and thus more manageable areas, on each you should subsequently write a paragraph; iii) briefly outline your argument or, perhaps, several possible arguments. An opening paragraph on these lines should help you to avoid the two most common errors in essay-writing, being irrelevant and giving a narrative account rather than an analysis.

Question 1. The starting point for this question must be a definition of socialism. The question also requires you to think on an international scale. So, a useful second step would be to identify those general factors that operated across frontiers as, for example, the rapid spread of industrialisation. Do bear in mind not all factors are equally significant. You might usefully suggest a broad scale of importance for the factors you mention. The question does pre-suppose that socialism did 'rise'; it would be perfectly valid to question and qualify this supposition. Remember the time frame of the question. The late 19th century refers to the last 35 years or so of the century. Finally, it is very important that you support your points with references, examples and arguments.

Question 2. It is always useful to work out what a question is 'getting at'. Here the implication is that there is a contradiction between being a Marxist party and taking an electoral approach. The first step would be to examine the political implications of being a Marxist party. Secondly, a comparison should be made between those implications and the practice of the SPD. This is likely to show that there is a contrast between Marxism and electoralism, between a belief in change by revolution and change through electoral success. The next task is to place this contrast in context by asking: what did Marx say about the process by which revolutions occur? If he argued that revolutions had to be actively promoted, that could point in one direction, whereas if he saw revolutions as developing automatically out of economic developments, that would point in another. It is also important to place you answer in context by looking at the SPD's view on this issue.

Question 3. The obvious starting point for this question is an outline of the International's policy on war prior to the outbreak of the First World War. The question clearly pre-supposes that the International failed to apply that policy. The bulk of your answer will, therefore, consist of an outline of the reasons it failed to oppose the war. As with all questions that require an examination of motivating factors you should attempt to evaluate the relative importance of the factors you describe. In your conclusion it would be appropriate to highlight the most important single factor, in your opinion. As always you should support your points with examples.

Question 4. This really falls neatly into three sections. Firstly, what was the split actually about? Secondly, what was the context of the split? Thirdly, what happened as a consequence of the split? In the first section you will be examining what the two sides were arguing about. In the second section you should attempt to relate the split to Russian political conditions, and to contemporary Marxist theory. Finally you need to assess the impact - both long- and short-term - that the split had on Russian politics and Marxist theory. This means that you must also refer to the chapter of this book, 'Socialism in Power in the Inter-War Years'.

Summary Diagram
Socialism Before 1914

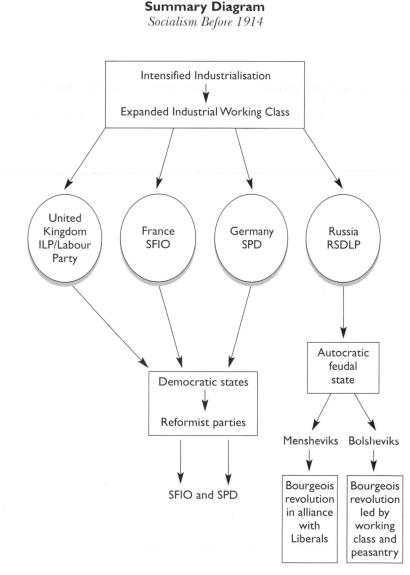

4 Socialism in Power in the Inter-War Years

1 Introduction

Until 1914 international socialism could be seen as a unified movement. After the outbreak of the First World War that apparent unity was shattered. The majority of socialists supported their national governments, but a significant minority, most notably the Bolsheviks, opposed the war. The Russian Revolution of October 1917 further fragmented international socialism. The successful Bolsheviks claimed to have solved the problem of how the transition from capitalism to socialism was to be effected. They further claimed that the experience of the First World War had discredited the old Socialist International. Subsequently, in 1919 the Bolsheviks, now renamed the Communist Party, established the Communist International (Comintern) to which newly formed communist parties around the world affiliated.

This process of polarisation had the effect of more clearly defining what socialism was, and how it was to be achieved. Broadly speaking, there emerged two distinct and opposing positions. Radical socialists were attracted to the revolutionary ideas of the Bolsheviks and joined the international communist movement. The departure of such people allowed the old socialist parties to become openly parliamentary parties with reformist programmes.

This chapter will outline the development of Soviet socialism within the Soviet Union as the touchstone of orthodoxy for the international communist movement. It will also consider the course followed by the German SPD up to 1933. The large SPD had not, despite its numerical strength, enjoyed political power prior to 1918. In that year the SPD took office in Germany, largely as a consequence of the military collapse. Once in office the party worked to establish a parliamentary democracy and contain the revolution that broke out in November of that year. The SPD, therefore, represents the polar opposite of Bolshevism and an examination of its development up to 1933 provides an example of reformist socialism at work.

In Britain the Labour Party had enjoyed only modest success before the First World War. Despite this, in 1924 the first Labour Government was formed. The chapter will consider what the experience of office revealed about the nature of British socialism.

The examination of these three examples has two purposes: firstly, to demonstrate the differences between revolutionary and reformist socialism and, secondly, to contrast varying national forms of socialism. It will also provide the opportunity to compare socialism in theory with socialism in power, raising the question, in some cases, as to whether certain regimes were really socialist at all.

2 Revolutionary Russia

In March 1917 the Tsar was forced to abdicate. The February Revolution, which brought this about, began as a series of protests against food and fuel shortages in Petrograd, the capital. At that stage even Bolshevik observers believed that the situation could be contained by the government. In the event Tsarism's fate was sealed by a failure to take resolute action against the protestors and the mutiny of the greater part of the Petrograd garrison. Faced with the disintegration of Tsarist authority, the *Duma* (Parliament) reluctantly, and against the wishes of the Tsar, formed a Provisional Government. The situation was further complicated by the creation of the Petrograd Soviet (council). This body consisted of delegates elected directly from workplaces and military units. The February Revolution therefore created two legislative bodies, a situation characterised as 'Dual Power'. Initially the Soviet, dominated by Mensheviks, supported the Provisional Government but, as we shall see, this situation did not continue. The Mensheviks supported the Provisional Government as part of their policy of promoting parliamentary government.

The Bolsheviks in Petrograd at first seemed inclined to follow the lead of the Mensheviks in, as they saw it, completing the *bourgeois* revolution. Yet their outlook changed dramatically with Lenin's return from exile. In a document subsequently known as the *April Theses* he declared his absolute opposition to the Provisional Government and its efforts to continue fighting the war. The objective of the Bolsheviks was, he declared, not a parliamentary republic 'but a Republic of Soviets of Workers, Agricultural Labourers and Peasant Deputies'.[1] At that time, when the Bolsheviks were relatively weak, Lenin's programme seemed wildly unrealistic.

After the collapse of Tsarism the Provisional Government failed to gather all of the reins of power in its hands. In the major centres within the factories, neighbourhoods and regiments, councils, or 'soviets', were formed. These local bodies in turn sent delegates to city-based soviets. Initially, the Petrograd and Moscow soviets were dominated by the Mensheviks. However, Lenin recognised that the soviets represented an alternative source of political power. Lenin described Russia as being in a situation of dual power with the workers' and peasants' soviets confronting the *bourgeois* Provisional Government.

In the aftermath of the February Revolution the Provisional Government progressively alienated large sections of the Russian people. The attempt to continue the war became very unpopular after the failure of the June 1917 offensive, the last offensive mounted by the Russian army. The peasants chafed at the refusal to break up the big estates and redistribute their lands. Urban workers continued to suffer food shortages. The Bolsheviks skilfully capitalised on these discontents. They promised the people 'Bread, Peace and Land', and they demanded 'All Power to the Soviets'. Bolshevik influence increased rapidly. Between February and October 1917 party membership rose from 10,000 to 300,000. They also gained control of the Moscow and Petrograd soviets. This increase in strength culminated in the October Revolution when they overthrew the Provisional Government and seized power. From that point onwards controversy accompanied every action taken by the Bolsheviks. They justified their seizure of power by reference to their majority within the soviets. However, Bolshevik support remained confined to the two principal cities, Petrograd and Moscow. The Bolsheviks clearly did not have the support of the mass of the Russian population. Neither was the October Revolution a popular uprising in the way that the February Revolution had been. Rather, it was a carefully orchestrated seizure of power. The use of the soviets to legitimise the Bolsheviks' actions was conditional on their dominance within them. Lenin had argued for the armed seizure of power as early as July 1917, at which point he had declared the soviets an irrelevance. The course of events after the October Revolution certainly lends credence to the idea that the Bolsheviks simply used the soviets as a pretext for their bid for power.

It is, therefore, easy to see why historians like Dmitri Volkogonov[2] have characterised the Bolshevik Revolution as a coup, that is an undemocratic military takeover. Commentators have subsequently been divided between those who explain communist curtailment of democratic freedoms as responses to difficult circumstances, and those who see them as integral elements of the essentially undemocratic nature of Bolshevik communism.

The communist regime did embody a number of contradictions. They had come to power demanding 'All Power to the Soviets' but in the aftermath of the revolution the soviets progressively lost power to the Communist Party until, by 1922 the Party was the centre of government, not the soviets. Prior to the revolution Lenin had proclaimed the need for a dictatorship of the proletariat, by which he meant rule by the workers not the *bourgeoisie*. However, again by 1922, the regime was more like a dictatorship of the Party. There were good reasons for this development: as a result of the civil war, which broke out in mid-1918, the working class largely disappeared. However, the rule of the soviets was never restored, even after the end of the civil war. In the *April Theses* Lenin had argued that the army should be disbanded and in its place the whole people should be armed. In the event the Red Army was created, with conventional ranks and military discipline, and it even employed ex-Tsarist officers. In 1918 the democratically elected Constituent Assembly was forcibly dissolved because it had an anti-Bolshevik majority. By 1922 all political parties and opposition factions within the Communist Party had been banned. It is therefore easy to see how a case can be made for the existence of a communist dictatorship.

The communist leadership were aware of the problems. Lenin

noted that the Party was substituting itself for the working class. Their problem, as they saw it, was that Marxist theory argued that socialist revolution would occur first in countries in which the working class formed the majority of the population. As that was not the case in Russia, Russian communists had depended on the outbreak of revolutions in Western Europe that would produce supportive communist regimes, with the kind of developed economies seen as necessary for the construction of socialism. Unfortunately, none of the revolutions that occurred in the West was successful. In this situation the Bolsheviks could either give up or take the draconian measures necessary for survival. In the event they opted for the latter, using repression to sustain their government. The difficulties of survival also changed the nature of the Party: it largely ceased to be a political body concerned with policy and ideology and became instead an arm of the government and military bureaucracy. This made it a very influential body. In 1922 Joseph Stalin became Party General Secretary, and thus the head of this powerful bureaucratic organisation.

In May 1922 illness removed Lenin from active politics. This initiated a power struggle for leadership of the Party, between Joseph Stalin and Leon Trotsky, a struggle that was eventually won by Stalin. This victory provides the focus for another on-going debate: did Stalin's policies represent a continuation of Lenin's, or were they a radical departure from those of the Bolshevik leader? On this issue historians take diametrically opposed positions. Dmitri Volkogonov states:

> The totalitarian Soviet state was built on Leninist principles ...[3]

Against this Moshe Lewin, speculating on what might have happened if Lenin had lived longer, declared:

> It is legitimate to believe that Lenin, acting in concert with Trotsky and others, would have been able to bring Soviet Russia through a less tragic, more rational and, for the cause of socialism, less compromising path.[4]

It is not possible to give a definitive answer to this question, but it is important to be aware of the debate because it reflects on the contemporary validity of Lenin's version of communism.

3 Stalin in Power

Between 1922 and 1928 Stalin entered into a series of alliances, all designed to deny Trotsky leadership of the Party. The crucial factor in Stalin's victory was his control of the Party machine. This enabled him to pack meetings with his own supporters and appointees, and to effectively deny his opponents a hearing within the Party.

One of the issues between Trotsky and Stalin was the management of the economy. During the civil war drastic measures had been taken to provide the cities and the Red Army with food. The government

ОРУЖИЕМ МЫ ДОБИЛИ ВРАГА
ТРУДОМ МЫ ДОБУДЕМ ХЛЕБ
ВСЕ ЗА РАБОТУ, ТОВАРИЩИ!

We have beaten the enemy by force of arms. We will earn our bread by labour.
Everything for work, comrades!

instituted the policy of war communism, which involved the forced requisitioning of foodstuffs by military units. This was not a popular policy with the peasantry, and could not continue for long in the face of their opposition. As the civil war ended in 1921 the Party introduced the New Economic Policy (NEP). This allowed the peasants to trade their produce for money, effectively reintroducing a capitalist element into the Soviet economy. It was successful in regenerating the circulation of foodstuffs, but it also encouraged the appearance of rich peasants (kulaks) and entrepreneurial middle men (Nepmen). Although seen as a temporary measure it was interpreted as a backward step by many in the Party. The fact that Soviet propaganda, like the poster on page 62, continued to emphasise the Party's attachment to the working class, and the benefits of industrialisation, gives an indication of the loyalties of Russian communists. Stalin and his allies were keen supporters of the NEP and continued it well after Lenin's death in 1924. Trotsky attacked the continuation of the NEP on two fronts. Firstly, because allowing the peasants to 'enrich themselves' limited the resources available for an increased programme of industrialisation. Secondly, because it encouraged the development of classes unsympathetic to the Revolution.

Another issue which divided the two rivals centred on the two slogans: 'Socialism in One Country' and 'World Revolution'. Trotsky argued that the Russian Revolution could only proceed to socialism with the assistance of other revolutionary regimes in more advanced countries. Against this Stalin asserted that the revolutionary wave in Europe had subsided and that consequently Russia had to construct socialism for itself. This flew in the face of Marxist orthodoxy, which argued that only advanced capitalist states possessed the economic development necessary to begin constructing socialism. However, the idea of 'Socialism in One Country' had a wide appeal within Russia. To a war-weary people it seemed to offer peace, without any dangerous foreign entanglements. It also appealed to nationalist feeling, as it seemed to support the view that the Russians did not need foreign aid to develop their state.

Given this analysis, defeats for the international communist movement strengthened Stalin's position. In the aftermath of the defeat of the Chinese communists at the hands of the Nationalists in 1927 - more evidence that the time was not ripe for world revolution - Stalin moved the expulsion of Trotsky and his Left Opposition grouping from the Party. Trotsky was sentenced to internal exile. Two years later he was deported from the Soviet Union.

In 1928 Stalin dramatically reversed his policies when he initiated the first Five Year Plan, and the collectivisation of agriculture. Individual peasant holdings were to be grouped together creating collective farms. Those who opposed this measure were labelled the 'Right Opposition' and defeated even more rapidly than the Trotskyists. Collectivisation was vigorously opposed by the peasants.

They slaughtered their livestock and burnt their crops to prevent their seizure. The government responded with incredible brutality. Collectivisation was enforced at the point of a gun, and resisters were often summarily executed. During the course of collectivisation Stalin declared his intention to 'liquidate the Kulaks as a class'. They were not allowed to join the collective farms but had their property confiscated and suffered mass deportations to Siberia. The short-term consequences of this process were reduced production, famine and death.

Collectivisation was an attempt to resolve the problem of food supplies for the cities by incorporating agriculture into a national system of planning. It was also a way of releasing resources, both material and human - ten million peasants left the land for the new industries of the Five Year Plan. In a speech made in 1931 Stalin gave the clearest explanation for the adoption of the plan.

> We are fifty or a hundred years behind the advanced countries. We must make good this lag in ten years. Either we do it or they crush us.[5]

The 'lag' was to be made good by the Plan, which was, in effect, a series of inflated production targets. Under the terms of the first Five Year Plan, for example, the production of pig iron was supposed to treble between 1928 and 1933. To achieve these targets millions of Russian workers were mobilised in an almost military fashion, though many of the new industrial workers genuinely believed they were building socialism and threw themselves enthusiastically into their work. Such people were the core of the Stakhanovite movement, named after the record-breaking miner, Alexi Stakhanov. Such workers were committed to the over-fulfilment of their production targets. Within the workplace a system of 'carrot and stick' was applied. Successful Stakhanovites enjoyed free holidays in state rest-homes and better quality accommodation. Those who failed to meet their targets found themselves accused of sabotage and drafted into forced labour units.

The first two Five Year Plans undoubtedly created the basis for an industrialised Soviet Union. However, they also created a severely over worked and badly housed labour force. This mixed experience has in turn led historians and analysts to different conclusions. Sidney and Beatrice Webb asked:

1 Will this new system of economic relationships and this new motivation of wealth production, prove permanently successful? For if it does, it will not only show the rest of the world how to abolish technological, and indeed all other mass unemployment, together with the devastating
5 alternation of commercial booms and slumps; but further, by opening the way to the maximum ultilization of human enterprise and scientific discovery in the service of humanity, it will afford the prospect of increase beyond all computation, alike of national wealth and of individual well-being.[6]

The Webbs concluded that this system would be permanently successful, and that, therefore, all these benefits would follow. Alan Wood, writing in 1990, took a very different view:

1   In human terms, however, the cost of this industrial progress was stag-
    gering. Machinery and equipment had at first to be bought from abroad,
    purchased with the revenue from exports of grain screwed from the
    collective farms. Food and consumer goods disappeared from the shops;
5   interminable queuing became a regular feature of daily existence;
    rationing was introduced; housing conditions in the over-crowded cities
    were appalling; wages failed to keep pace with rocketing prices.[7]

It is possible to argue that, despite the suffering they caused, collectivisation and industrialisation were both necessary developments. Yet the same cannot be said for the Great Terror that Stalin unleashed in 1934. This began after the assassination of Sergei Kirov, head of the Leningrad Party organisation. Stalin used this event as a pretext to 'uncover' a massive anti-Soviet conspiracy. According to the show trials which began in 1936 virtually all the original Bolshevik leaders had been actively plotting Stalin's death and the destruction of the Soviet system. During the trials the veterans 'confessed' to the most preposterous charges and received the only sentence possible - death. By 1940, the entire 1917 leadership of the Bolshevik Party, bar Stalin, was dead.

Away from the spotlight of the trials millions suffered execution or imprisonment in Soviet concentration camps. A number of explanations have been offered for the Terror. For example, the removal of the old Bolsheviks and their replacement by Stalin's appointees reinforced his position by reducing the possibility of opposition. Similarly, the creation of an atmosphere of terror, in which individuals had to watch their every word for fear of the consequences, made the appearance of a grassroots opposition unlikely. The consequences of the Terror are clear: the Soviet Union's political and military leadership was decimated.

The enormity of Stalin's crimes has produced endless debate as to his motivations. For some, like the Russian writer Alexander Solzhenitsyn, the answer is simple: Stalin was a logical development of communist tyranny. For him what separates Lenin and Stalin is a question of degree, not principle. Trotsky argued that Stalin represented the interests of the Party bureaucracy, a parasitic grouping that created a privileged lifestyle for itself. It is certainly true that the bureaucracy was better fed, better clothed and better housed than the rest of Soviet society. Stalin even made a speech in 1934 attacking those who believed socialism meant equality. One of the central assumptions of Marxism was, he argued, that under socialism each would contribute according to his abilities, and receive according to his needs.

> Marxism starts out with the assumption that people's abilities and requirements are not, and cannot be, equal in quality or in quantity, either in the period of socialism or in the period of communism.[8]

Given that Marxism believed that socialism could only exist in a situation of material plenty, Stalin's views on equality are, at best, dubious.

Isaac Deutscher noted that Stalin, unlike other Bolshevik leaders, had little direct knowledge of the advanced states of Western Europe. Deutscher further argued that Stalin was much more influenced by the autocratic methods of Tsarism than by the democracy of the West. This, it is argued, inclined Stalin to view policy as an administrative not a political issue. In other words, decisions had to be enacted not with the consent of the people but despite them. This is not an exhaustive review of the analyses offered on the question of Stalin's motives, but it does give an indication of the nature of the problem.

4 Stalin and the Outside World

Stalin's policies did not simply affect the Soviet Union. Since 1919 the leadership of the Communist International had been based in Moscow. After securing his position Stalin used the Comintern as an agency of Soviet foreign policy. This resulted in the international communist movement undergoing a series of dramatic policy zig-zags. When in 1939, for example, the Soviet Union signed a non-aggression pact with Nazi Germany, European communist parties switched, virtually overnight, from supporting the democracies against Germany to denouncing them as aggressor states. Such was the prestige of the October Revolution that committed communists around the world were prepared to accept these abrupt changes. Nor were communists the only people to view Stalin positively. During the 1930s, in a period of economic slump, the Soviet Union presented itself as a growing, vibrant economy, free from unemployment. This attracted the attention of many Western socialists and liberals and inclined them to give Stalin the benefit of the doubt. Of course, those who visited Russia only saw what their hosts wished them to see.

By the end of the 1930s, three Five Year Plans had turned Russia into an industrial power, but at a tremendous human cost. For many in the West the Soviet Union was a beacon of what could be achieved by centralised state planning. It also represented for its supporters the realisation of socialism. However, apart from state ownership and control of industry and agriculture there was little that conformed to Marx's views on socialism. The armed forces were massive and there were no plans to replace them with an armed people. The division of labour, particularly between physical and intellectual work, had been intensified, rather than abolished, and was buttressed by differential wage rates. Soviet society was not a society of plenty, but one of severe shortages, particularly of consumer goods. Such goods as were available were unequally distributed, with the bulk going to members of the state bureaucracy. There was no direct, participatory democracy; instead there was the undemocratic rule of the Party. In the 1930s these features, and the massive state repression that accompanied them, were largely masked from Western eyes. When the real nature of Soviet society became known to a wider audience, after the Second World War, it would play a large part in the discrediting of socialism that such a society had been upheld as the embodiment of socialism.

5 German Social Democracy

By the autumn of 1918 Germany was staring defeat in the face. The failure of its 1918 offensive and the arrival of increasing numbers of American troops convinced the German leadership that they could not win. In the face of growing domestic discontent Germany's rulers needed a government that would be able both to negotiate a peace and maintain order in Germany. Hitherto Germany had been a limited democracy with real political control vested in the Emperor. The Reichstag (parliament) acted as a consultative body and could be ignored by ministers who were directly appointed by the Crown. The decision was now taken to transform Germany into a full parliamentary democracy, that is, to make government answerable to the Reichstag. As the largest single party in the Reichstag was the SPD, this necessarily meant a governing role for the Party for the first time in its history. It seems likely that the German military hoped that the main effect of this change would be to pin the blame for Germany's defeat on to the socialists. Whether or not the military had this degree of foresight, the SPD leadership were subsequently labelled the 'November Criminals' for accepting the armistice by Germany's political right.

In November mutiny broke out in the Baltic fleet. The sailors refused to sail out to face a pointless death before the guns of the British fleet. The mutiny rapidly spread from Kiel becoming, in the process, a revolution. Within days all the major German cities were affected. The revolutionaries deposed the military authorities and elected councils of workers and soldiers to rule in their place. These councils bore more than a passing resemblance to the Russian soviets, and led many to view this movement as more radical than it was in reality. The German Communist Party (KPD) was not formed until the very end of 1918 and even then its forces were very small. It seems likely that the great bulk of the revolutionaries were SPD supporters, and their principal concern was the question of the war and the rule of the German militarists.

In response to this development Friedrich Ebert, the SPD leader, declared:

> Unless the Kaiser abdicates the social revolution is inevitable. But I will have none of it, I hate it like sin.[9]

The abdication of the Kaiser and the appointment of Ebert as the first Social Democrat chancellor of Germany occurred in quick succession. The key point to note here is that the SPD saw its role as being to halt the revolution. How was it that a still self-avowedly Marxist party could arrive at such a position? As we have seen, the SPD had long been a party within which a day-to-day reformism was combined with an espousal of a distant revolutionary goal (see page 41). This paradox became more marked during the war. On the one hand the SPD, although not admitted to government, was consulted by the government on questions relating to production and industrial efficiency; Party leaders began to feel that they were beginning, at least, to approach the portals of power. Yet at the same time the more radical elements of the Party left it. Rosa Luxemburg and Karl Liebknecht, the Party's most prominent Marxist revolutionaries, spent much of the war in prison because of their opposition to it. For many years the SPD had dominated the Reichstag in terms of numbers, but had been denied access to power by the imperial constitution. The reforms of 1918 changed all that and, to the SPD's pragmatic leadership, appeared to give the Party all it had ever wanted. For all these reasons the Party pledged itself in 1918 to 'save Germany from Bolshevism'.

What did such a commitment mean in practice? What could the new SPD government do about the revolutionary wave sweeping Germany? Initially, they could not oppose it outright. This was because they had no forces with which to do so. Troops returning from the front, after the Armistice, simply wanted to go home. The first tactic of the SPD leadership was, therefore, to place itself at the head of the revolutionary movement. On 10 November, at a mass meeting of delegates from the workers' and soldiers' councils, the government was restructured, becoming a council of People's Commissars made up of six members. Immediately after this meeting People's Commissar Ebert had a telephone conversation with General Groener. Out of this conversation came the Ebert-Groener agreement. This pledged the military to support the republican government in return for which the government was to leave the existing-military leadership and its privileges intact. Between November and January 1919 the military, in co-operation with the SPD leadership, made its preparations for the suppression of the revolution. To justify their hostility to the council movement the SPD leadership continually described it as Bolshevik. They further argued that the National Assembly of Workers' and Soldiers' Councils saw itself as an alternative to the National Assembly which was to be elected in January. The SPD leaders were aware that comparisons could be made between the Russian Constituent Assembly and their own projected National Assembly; and, of course, they knew that the Bolsheviks had soon sent the democratically elected Assembly packing. However, a key element for a German 'October Revolution'

The Council of People's Representatives

was missing: there was no disciplined revolutionary party with a mass following. Liebknecht and Luxemburg did not even have seats on the National Assembly of Workers' and Soldiers' Councils.

Indeed, far from seeing itself in opposition to the National Assembly, the council movement had actually voted to bring forward the date of its election. According to one German historian, workers' and soldiers' councils 'confined their activities primarily to the maintenance of order'.[10] The hostility of the SPD leadership seems more a reflection of their limited political ambitions than of a real Bolshevik threat.

In January, following clashes over the Christmas holiday between military units for and against the revolution, demonstrations were organised. The demonstrations rapidly turned into a trial of strength, and the armed demonstrators occupied key positions within the capital. However, this movement received no clear leadership and began to waver. At this point the military intervened and, with great brutality, suppressed the revolution. Berlin saw many summary executions, including those of Karl Liebknecht and Rosa Luxemburg. This was the bloody backdrop for the creation of the Weimar Republic, so called because its constitution was framed in the city of Weimar.

6 The SPD and the Weimar Republic

For the SPD leadership Weimar was a triumph. In the elections of January 1919 the SPD took 40 per cent of the vote, and the chancellorship. However, although it was the biggest single party it did not have an outright majority and could only rule in coalition with other parties. Between 1919 and 1923 the SDP governed Germany through a variety of coalitions. This clearly limited the Party's scope for radical redistribution of wealth and property (although it is possible to ask how far they were actually committed to radical change at this stage). The 1920 Works Council Law required factories employing more than 20 workers to elect a works' council. These councils were to 'look after the economic interests of the employees' *and* 'support the employer in the fulfilment of the establishment's purpose'. Such a dual role clearly could only be based on a rejection of the class struggle: indeed it logically presumed a common interest between employer and employee. This could be explained away as the consequence of being in coalition with non-socialist parties. However, the same kind of thinking is evident during those periods when the Party was out of government. In 1927, for example, the Party's leading theorist argued that since contemporary capitalism operated in a more rational fashion than in the 19th century, it was possible to detect within it:

... the substitution of the principle of free competition by the socialist principle of planned production.[11]

The economic policy of the SDP was extremely conservative in these years. Their Marxist heritage taught them that socialism could only be built on the basis of prosperity. Their commitment to democratic methods, combined with their minority position when in government, meant that their policies were driven by the need to restore the prosperity of capitalism. As they lacked any distinctive economic programme to achieve this, they simply applied conventional economic cures: a defence of balanced budgets, that is making sure that expenditure did not exceed income; a defence of the gold standard, that is linking the currency to the value of gold; and, finally a reliance on the operation of the market to restore the economy. In the difficult circumstances of the 1920s and '30s the SPD was, at best, ambivalent about what it was trying to do. The contradictions within the Party were very clearly summed up at the 1931 congress:

> Standing at the sickbed of capitalism is our position … that of a physician who wishes to heal the patient? Or of the joyful heir who can hardly wait to see the end and would really love to accelerate it with a little poison?[12]

In the event the SPD seemed more inclined to play the physician than the joyful patient.

The timidity of the SPD did affect its popularity. In 1919 it polled 11,509,000 votes, but this proved to be a peak that it never achieved again. Many of its disillusioned supporters turned to the newly formed Communist Party (KPD). By 1920, just a year after its formation, the KPD had a membership of 200,000. In 1930 the SPD polled 8,577,700 votes compared with 4,592,000 for the KPD. This was still a combined vote for the working-class parties of over 13 million but, while the SPD were fervent supporters of the Weimar Republic, the communists worked equally fervently for its overthrow. Furthermore, after 1929 the communists devoted a great deal of energy, on the instructions of their Soviet leaders, to attacking the SPD. This mutual antagonism ruled out any formal co-operation against the growing threat posed by Nazism.

In normal circumstances it might be expected that democratic reformist parties would have to modify their principles and programmes once in office. Unfortunately for the SPD times were not normal in Germany between 1918 and 1933. The Weimar Republic had been created, in part, by the bloody endeavours of those who opposed everything it stood for. The suppression of the democratic council movement meant that there was not a thorough reform of Germany's institution and that many important positions continued to be occupied by those who detested the republic and all that was associated with it.

The thousands of officials in the civil service and army who thought like this did their work at best without conviction and at worst actively sabotaged the efforts of the republic. The absolute failure to come to grips with the economic crises that affected Germany in these years further embittered much of German society towards the republic. In 1919 the combined vote of the working-class parties was 13,826,000. In November 1932 they received over 13 million votes. The figures can be read in two ways: on the one hand, throughout this period socialist parties took over one-third of the national vote; on the other hand, the figures indicate a failure to advance. It would seem likely that the socialist parties retained the support of their working-class constituencies but failed to make significant gains within the middle classes. They increasingly turned to a right-wing radical alternative, Nazism.

The final drama of social democracy began with the downfall of the last Social Democratic chancellor in 1930. During the 21 months of this coalition government unemployment had risen rapidly. The government had also negotiated the Young Plan, which had finally fixed the timetable for Germany's reparations payments. Reparations were payments for the damage that Germany had caused in the First World War, flowing from Germany's acceptance of responsibility for the war, as set down in the Treaty of Versailles. Nazi propaganda neatly linked unemployment to the deeply resented Versailles settlement:

> ... 18.7 per cent of the working population of Germany is unemployed, and only 1.5 per cent of the French working classes. What is the cause of this? Reparations, which have enriched France as much as they have impoverished the Reich.[13]

Reparations was a thorny subject with the SPD: they were, after all, the product of a treaty brought about by the hated 'November Criminals', the SDP leadership that had ended the war in 1918. The Social Democratic government collapsed because the People's Party withdrew their support. The next chancellor found it impossible to obtain a parliamentary majority, and so bypassed the Reichstag, and ruled by issuing decrees directly from his office. At this point Weimar democracy effectively ended. The SPD gave their support to this government, despite its policy of driving down the living standards of the lower classes, because it was better than the alternative. It was also part of the SPD's policy of placing national above class interests. In 1932, Franz von Papen, a member of the Harzburg Front, which included the Nationalists and the Nazis, became chancellor.

Papen continued to rule by decree. One of his first decrees was directed at the Social Democratic government of Prussia. Weimar Germany was a federal state within which each state had its own parliament and government. Prussia was the largest and most polit-ically significant of the states; Berlin, the federal capital, was in Prussia. The Social Democrats had dominated the government of Prussia for some time. On 20 July 1932 Papen published a decree which dismissed the Prussian government, and appointed himself as Commissar of the Reich in Prussia. This action was designed to forestall the difficulties that Papen's right-wing government was likely to experience with a Social Democratic Prussia.

This was a decisive moment for German social democracy. Papen's action was clearly undemocratic and undermined the very basis of SPD political practice. On the face of it the Prussian SPD seemed well positioned to resist. The chief of the police and his immediate superior, the Minister of the Interior, were both Social Democrats. They commanded a well-armed force of 100,000 men. In the event of resistance they could count on the support of the mainly SDP, republican militia. Against them would be ranged the 100,000 men of the regular army and the nationalist militia. Any confrontation would be bloody but, with the assistance of the trade unions, the Social Democrats at least stood a chance. In the event the issue was decided not by force of arms, but by the ideological convictions of the SPD. The day after the Social Democrat ministers were physically ejected from their offices the *Vorwarts*, the SDP paper, appeared with the headline:

> Everyone to the Polls on the 31st! Thus will the politically conscious working class of Germany put an end to the regime of the Barons.[14]

The 'regime of the Barons', Papen's government, deployed arbitrary decrees against the SPD, and the SPD responded by placing its faith in the electoral process; clearly the players in this game were using different rules. In January 1933, President Hindenburg appointed Adolf Hitler, leader of the Nazi Party, chancellor. The SDP reacted to this in much the same way as they had to Papen's 1932 decree: they attempted to adapt to the new government. In March, as part of their efforts to appease the Nazis, the SPD left the Labour and Socialist International. It all came to nought for in June 1933 the SPD became a banned organisation, its properties seized and its leaders imprisoned or exiled.

Two inter-related processes can be identified to explain the fate of German social democracy. In the short-term after 1918, the Party was operating in an extremely unfavourable environment. The personnel occupying key positions within the state bureaucracy and army were deeply hostile to the democratic republican regime. In periods of stability the republic could operate with a measure of success, but in periods of economic difficulty, particularly after 1929, the groupings that opposed the republic at a popular level rapidly gained ground. Every increase in unemployment brought fresh recruits and more votes for the Nazis. When the Nazi mass movement and the anti-republican establishment linked up, as they did in 1933, that fate of social democracy was sealed. The SDP learnt to their cost that democratic socialist parties can only operate when their opponents are prepared to operate democratically as well.

The second process at work concerns the long-term development of the SPD. As early as the 1890s there was a growing awareness within the SPD that there was a contradiction between the Party's daily political practice and its long-term goal of socialist transformation. Since that date socialist transformation had moved even further into the future. German social democracy as it emerged from the First World War had very modest objectives, partly because all of the governments in which it participated in 1919-23 and 1928-30 were coalitions with non-socialist parties. The SDP did promote significant measures of social reform, like the extension of social insurance, but it did not at any point look like effecting a socialist transformation. There were elements that claimed that capitalism was evolving into socialism and that, therefore, class conflict should replaced by class co-operation. However, there were still those who kept in mind, in whatever form, the notion of class conflict. The difficulties that the SPD faced were vividly illustrated by a speech to the 1925 Party congress:

1   In essence the Social Democrats are, and remain, the advocate of the
    poor, the workers and the disinherited. We must use all our power in
    public life to defend the vital interests of the working people and of the
    innocent victims of the capitalist economy against the patronage of
5   property. Thus, when we are in opposition, our demands must not
    exceed those limits which we have to honour if we were in power.[15]

Here the existence of separate class interests is recognised, but all that can be offered the 'innocent victims of the capitalist economy' are the limited measures that the Social Democrats could take within the constraints of a coalition. The SPD was evolving into a reformist party at a time when the possibilities for social reform were extremely limited. At the same time it had not fully shrugged off its political heritage but was unable to present its followers with a clear reformist path to socialism. The experience, then, of the SPD between 1918 and 1933 was that of a confused party, limited in its aspirations and unable to present its supporters with a way forward in the face of the twin threats of fascism and economic collapse.

It is one of the ironies of history that the leading party in the government that banned the SDP should also describe itself as socialist. Within the programme of the National Socialist German Workers' Party - the full name of the Nazi Party - there were measures that, at least, seemed left wing in nature. They demanded, for example, the nationalisation of all large companies and the abolition of all unearned income. Yet the real test of any organisation is what it does, rather than what it says, and once in power the Nazis totally ignored all of the socialist elements in their programme. Hitler made his views clear in the early 1930s in discussions held with left-wing Nazis. When asked about the social revolution he responded:

1   There are no revolutions except racial revolutions: there cannot be a
    political, economic, or social revolution - always and only it is the
    struggle of the lower stratum of inferior race against the dominant
    higher race, and if this higher race has forgotten the law of its existence,
5   then it loses the day.[16]

Asked what he would do about Krupps, a major industrial corpora-
tion, he replied:

1 Of course I should leave it alone. Do you think that I should be so mad
   as to destroy Germany's economy? Only if people should fail to act in
   the interests of the nation, then - and only then - would the State intervene. But for that you do not need an expropriation ... you need only
5 a strong State.[17]

Here Hitler did keep his word, large companies like Krupps were not
nationalised. Hitler's socialism, then, involved no conception of a
class struggle, and had no plans for major shifts in ownership once he
had gained power. Germany under Hitler was as much a capitalist
power as it was before his accession to power. At most, it would seem,
Hitler's socialism was a useful recruiting tool in the pioneering days of
the movement.

7 Labour into Office

At the onset of the First World War the Joint Board of Labour and the
TUC declared an industrial truce, committing the Labour movement
to unconditional support for the war-effort. Many within the
Independent Labour Party were unhappy about this, but their opposition to the war came from a variety of positions and had little impact
on the movement as a whole. When it became clear that this would be
a long-drawn-out conflict the British government moved to use the
Labour movement as part of its drive to increase production. In 1915
three Labour MPs were given government positions. At the end of
1916 Arthur Henderson, the leader of the PLP, entered the war
cabinet.

The acceptance of government office considerably raised Labour's
political profile. However, it was not a move without certain dangers.
Wartime working conditions were harsh, hours were long, certain
foods were in short supply and prices rose dramatically. The official
Labour movement, committed to the war effort, was not in a position
to take direct action to remedy these problems. Discontent within
engineering was particularly intense. Here, the introduction of large
numbers of unskilled and semi-skilled workers was added to the other
sources of discontent. Skilled engineers felt that their privileged position would be permanently undermined by this development. These
issues occasioned a number of large-scale strikes during the war. In
the absence of official leadership these strikes were often led by shop
stewards with very left-wing views, many of them active syndicalists
before the war. These shop stewards did not confine their activities to
fighting for wage increases, they sought to develop an alternative
form of industrial organisation - the workplace committee. These
aimed to organise all the workers, regardless of grade, within any one
establishment. In 1917 one of these shop stewards published a plan

for a nationally co-ordinated system of workplace committees. These developments raised the possibility that Labour might lose its grass-roots support to more radical individuals and organisations.

Official Labour was certainly aware of the development of this rank and file movement. The Labour Party archives contain an unsigned, confidential memorandum, written in 1917, that discusses ways of combating the shop stewards. Some historians have argued that it was this domestic threat combined with the outbreak of revolution in Russia that led to Labour's partial disengagement from the coalition. Arthur Henderson resigned from the government in 1917, after a trip to Russia convinced him that a negotiated peace was necessary to prevent the Bolsheviks overthrowing the Provisional Government. The following year the Labour Party adopted a constitution which committed the Party to socialism. The key clause in the new constitution stated that the purpose of the Party was:

1 To secure for producers by hand or brain the full fruits of their industry and the most equitable distribution thereof that may be possible, upon the basis of the Common Ownership of the Means of Production and the best obtainable system of popular administration and control of
5 each industry or service.[18]

The adoption of this constitution has generated considerable debate as to its real significance. Some have seen it as reflecting a general radicalisation of British society, as a consequence of the war; others have claimed it was a ploy to head off the development of a radical left-wing movement outside the Labour Party. Whatever way one reads it, it is clear that the socialism it offered lacked clear definition. Indeed, in a leaflet issued in 1918, Sidney Webb, the consitution's principal author, made clear that this was a deliberate intention:

… it is a Socialism which is no more specific than a definite repudiation of the individualism that characterised all the political parties of the past generation, and that still dominates the House of Commons.[19]

This deliberate vagueness, combined with the qualifying phrase 'that may be possible' in its socialist clause, makes it difficult to tease out what the new constitution actually committed the Party to. This can only be clarified by looking at the record of Labour in office.

The first Labour government came into office in 1924. As a minority government, it was not even the largest party in the Commons; it depended on the support of the Liberals in the Commons. This minority position was often used, then and now, to explain this government's very modest achievements. However, it is also clear that, regardless of this, the Labour Party's leadership was politically inclined to moderation. Even before taking office the Party leadership had been at pains to distance itself from industrial militancy. The outlook of the Labour government was described by Philip Snowden, the first Labour Chancellor of the Exchequer:

1   A Labour Government would undoubtedly disappoint its critics in one
very important and vital respect. It would not be a class government. I
know that there will be strong pressure from certain quarters to use a
Labour Government to serve the interests and meet the claims of
5   certain sections of Labour. That and not the opposition of capitalists and
financial interests will be its greatest difficulty.[20]

A government committed to presenting only measures that would be
successful, that is win Liberal support, and, furthermore, a government that identified its own left wing as its principal enemy - such was
the nature of the first Labour government. In the circumstances it is
not surprising that this government only achieved a few, relatively
minor, reforms.

The record of the second Labour government, elected in 1929, was,
if anything, worse than that of the first. This minority government
came into office at the outset of the Great Depression and was immediately confronted with spiralling unemployment. This was most
evident in the areas dominated by Britain's old staple industries, the
same areas that provided Labour with the bulk of its electoral
support. However, Labour's economic policy was dominated by the
ideas of 19th-century Liberalism. In times of economic crisis,
according to this doctrine, governments should cut expenditure. So,
at a time when the demand for unemployment benefit was rapidly
increasing, and when left-wingers in the Party were demanding public
works schemes to give work to the unemployed, the Labour leadership was committed to cutting back on spending.

The situation came to a head in 1931 when, faced with a projected
budget deficit of £120 million, the government was forced to consider
major economies. The situation was compounded when French and
American banks made clear that no further loans would be advanced
unless major cut-backs in government expenditure occurred.
Everyone in the Cabinet was committed to balancing the budget, that
is matching expenditure to income, but it proved impossible for them
to agree where the cuts should fall. Cuts in unemployment benefit
were particularly hard for many to swallow. In the face of this disagreement Ramsay MacDonald, the Party leader, resigned as Labour Prime
Minister, and was promptly reappointed as Prime Minister at the head
of a Conservative-dominated coalition. This government argued the
need for equality of sacrifice in the national interest. The Labour
Party was keenly aware, as the poster below shows, that an equal level
of sacrifice, including a 10 per cent cut in unemployment benefit,
would not be equally felt. In the general election of 1931 Labour was
almost annihilated, its parliamentary representation falling from 288
seats to fewer than 60.

Labour's problem was that it had largely adopted the gradualist
perspectives of the Fabians. This view argued that socialism was the
inevitable direction in which society would move. However, this

movement would, it was argued, proceed in a piecemeal fashion over a long period of time. Hence, the introduction of old age pensions before the First World War could be seen as part of the move towards socialism, and so too could the Wheatley Housing Act of 1924 (which increased the provision of council housing). Socialism was inevitable, but it was a long way off, and could only be approached very slowly. In the meantime as a self-proclaimed national party Labour had to maintain the prosperity of the national economy, which it attempted to do with orthodox Liberal economics.

In the extreme circumstances of the inter-war years Labour simply was not equipped, in an ideological sense, to offer its supporters anything but the cold comfort of a balanced budget, and the prospect of socialism in the distant future. Ramsay MacDonald was, when he and a few colleagues joined the coalition, simply following through

From "PLEBS" (the Organ of the N.C.L.C.)

Labour Party election poster 1931

the logic of Labour's position, a point he himself made in a general election broadcast. At the same time the crisis of 1931 demonstrated the considerable weaknesses of Labour's socialism.

It would be unbalanced not to mention those in the Labour Party who opposed the approach of the leadership. In 1924, for example, the ILP had argued that the government should press ahead with bold measures of social reform. They believed that the parliamentary defeat of such measures would place the Labour Party in a strong position to fight a general election. In 1932, disillusioned, the ILP disaffiliated from the Labour Party. They left behind a rump of members who formed the Socialist League. On paper the League sounded very radical, basing its arguments on the belief that capitalism was at the point of total collapse. In the early 1930s its members successfully proposed resolutions that committed the Labour Party to immediately implement socialist measures when elected into office. Yet the League was marginalised after 1934 when a measure of economic recovery appeared to make its arguments redundant.

Another consequence of the post-1934 recovery was the emergence of a group of young Labour economists who devoted themselves to developing practical measures of socialist planning that could be implemented in the short-term, within a capitalist economy. Their efforts culminated in the publication of *Labour's Immediate Programme* in 1937. This was a short-term programme designed for implementation immediately upon assuming office. It was an alternative to the 'catastrophism' of the Socialist League, and the extreme gradualism and Liberal economics of the MacDonald era.

In the event this development did not bear fruit until 1945. Overall, the 1930s were a bleak period for Labour, and it won only 154 seats in the 1935 general election, compared with 288 in 1929. Ironically, considering its constant assertion that it was a national not a class-based party, it failed to advance outside its working-class industrial strongholds. It was not until 1945 that Labour received a significant middle-class vote.

8 Conclusion

The record of socialist movements in power in the inter-war period is, to say the least, a mixed one. In Europe's two principal industrial powers, Great Britain and Germany, mass socialist parties did enjoy periods in office, something that had not seemed remotely possible before the First World War. However, neither the German SPD nor the British Labour Party achieved majorities in their respective parliaments. Both, it could be said, enjoyed office but not power. It is also the case that neither party made any real attempt substantially to alter the balance of power and wealth. Clearly, it could be argued that their lack of majorities made it impossible for them to implement radical programmes. There is, though, abundant evidence that neither was temperamentally inclined towards radicalism. Philip Snowden, for example, claimed before Labour even took office that a Labour government's principal problem would be left-wing members of the Labour Party. Similarly, the SPD leadership found itself more in sympathy with Germany's military elite, than with supporters of the Workers' and Soldiers' Council movement. From different traditions and histories these two reformist parties evolved in a similar direction. They were both reforming parliamentary parties content to work within existing political structures. Their common problem was that neither was equipped to deal with the extreme circumstances of the 1930s. Both were overwhelmed by events beyond their powers to control, the German SPD rather more seriously than British Labour. A key part of their problem was that they adopted a reformist strategy, but they did not, until much later, develop a reformist economic and political programme. Consequently, once in office, both parties tended to fall back on existing economic orthodoxies.

The social democratic parties of Western Europe were also anxious to distinguish themselves from the international communist movement, and to demonstrate that they were national, not class-based, parties, and that they were constitutional and not revolutionary. The Soviet Union clearly was the product of major readjustments of wealth and authority. It was also, in the course of the 1930s, creating the basis for an industrial economy. Equally, however, it was characterised by a complete lack of political democracy. During the course of the civil war (1919-1921), the Communist Party had substituted itself for the vanishing working class and, eventually, Stalin substituted himself for the Communist Party. The advances made in the Soviet Union were achieved at a terrific cost in lives and suffering. In a world of economic collapse, war and advancing fascism this was not the key point for Western observers, the vast majority of whom were ignorant of the real nature of the Soviet Union anyway. With the benefit of hindsight we now know that the intensely repressive Soviet Union bore no resemblance at all to Marx's vision of communism. That it proved so attractive during the 1930s to Western intellectuals is, in part, an indication of the disappointment felt at the record of democratic socialism.

References

1   V.I. Lenin, 'The Tasks of the Proletariat in the Present Revolution (1917)', in *Lenin Selected Works Vol.2* (Progress Publishers, Moscow, 1970), p. 45
2   Dmitri Volkogonov, *Lenin. Legacy and Life* (Harper Collins, 1994), pp. 155-6
3   Ibid., p. 448
4   Moshe Lewin, *Lenin's Last Struggle* (Faber and Faber, 1969), pp. 139-40.
5   Issac Deutscher, *Stalin* (Penguin, 1966), p. 328.
6   Sidney and Beatrice Webb, *Soviet Communism: A New Civilisation?* (Longmans, Green and Co., 1935), p. 602.

7   Alan Wood, *Stalin and Stalinism* (Routledge, 1990), p. 34.
8   Sidney and Beatrice Webb, *Soviet Communism: A New Civilisation?* p. 702.
9   Sebastian Haffner, *Failure of a Revolution. Germany 1918/19* (André Deutsch, 1973), p. 65.
10 Helga Grebing, *History of the German Labour Movement* (Berg, 1985), p. 103.
11 W.L.Guttsman, *The German Social Democratic Party 1875-1933* (George Allen and Unwin, 1981), p. 319.
12 Walter Kendall, *The Labour Movement in Europe* (Allen Lane, 1975), p. 104.
13 A. Ramos Oliveira, *A People's History of Germany* (Gollancz, 1942), p. 156.
14 Ibid., p. 162
15 Grebing, *History of the German Labour Movement*, p. 133.
16 Alan Bullock, *Hitler and Stalin: Parallel Lives* (HarperCollins, 1991), p. 190.
17 Ibid., p. 190.
18 David Howell, *British Social Democracy* (Croom Helm, 1980), p. 32.
19 Sidney Webb, *The New Constitution of the Labour Party* (Labour Party, 1918).
20 J.T. Murphy, *Preparing for Power* (Pluto Press, 1972), p. 221.

Source-based questions: 'Socialism in Power in the Inter-War Years'

1   Two views of Soviet industrialisation.
Read the extracts from the Webbs and Alan Wood on pages 64-65.
a) How far does the Webbs' reference to unemployment help to explain their enthusiasm for Soviet methods? (3 marks)
b) What do the Webbs mean by the phrase 'new motivation of wealth creation'? (4 marks)
c) Does Wood's account directly contradict that of the Webbs'? (5 marks)
d) Do you find the Webbs' or Wood's account the more useful? Explain your answer. (7 marks)
e) How far does the difference in dates of publication explain the differences between the two extracts? (6 marks)

2   Political propaganda in the inter-war years
Study the posters that appear on pages 62 and 78.
a) What do the images in the Soviet poster tell you about the type of labour that the artist thinks most important for the Soviet Union's future? (4 marks)
b) What point is the Labour Party poster making? (4 marks)
c) What do these posters tell you about the political parties that produced them? (6 marks)
d) How do the posters relate to the situations in which they were produced? (6 marks)

Hints and Advice

Visual images, like posters, are designed to be taken in at a glance. Consequently a real effort has to be made in order to analyse how they are designed to work - that is, to understand who they are aimed at, the views they represent, and the nature of the appeal they are making.

a) Posters are visual sources. The images they contain are designed to have a lasting impression. The images also reinforce and inter-pret the text of the poster. How, then do these images interpret this text? What type of labour is emphasised here, and what type of future is envisaged for the Soviet Union?

b) This question is asking you to translate into words the visual message of the poster. What, for example, does the relative posi-tion of the figures tell you? What does it tell you about Labour's view of society? Does it say anything about Labour's view of its opponents?

c) This question requires you to think who is being addressed by these posters, and what they are being asked to do. The nature of the task will directly relate both to the social position of the audi-ence and to the nature of the political parties that produced the posters.

d) This question is asking you to relate the posters to the situation in which they were produced, the Soviet Union in 1921 and Great Britain in 1931. The question is asking you how the posters illu-minate key features of those times and places.

Summary Diagram
Socialism in Power in the Inter-War Years

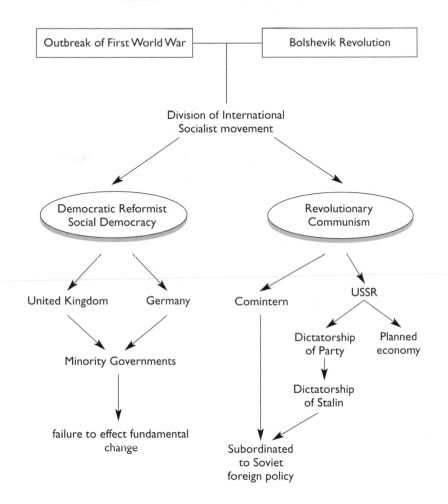

5 Mao and China

1 Introduction

China presents students of communism with a number of issues for consideration. Firstly, China, the second major country to experience a communist revolution, was a predominantly peasant society when in 1949 the People's Republic of China (PRC) was established. This immediately raises the question of how this peasant-based revolution can be reconciled with Marxist doctrine, which gives the leading role in the socialist revolution to the working class. Secondly, China, unlike Russia, was the direct victim of imperialism. Throughout the 19th century a variety of powers had used their military superiority to force China to grant them territorial and trading concessions. By 1900 50 'treaty ports' under foreign control dominated China's coastline. In the 1930s the Japanese launched a direct military assault on China. After transforming the outlying province of Manchuria into the puppet-state of Manchukuo, they turned their attention to the bulk of China in 1937. These foreign incursions meant that China's communists did not simply face the task of social revolution but also had to confront the problem of national survival. Finally, when formed in 1921 the Chinese Communist Party (CCP) was not simply a national party but part of an international movement, an affiliated section of the Communist International. This organisation, based in Moscow, derived enormous prestige from the successful Bolshevik Revolution. Initially formed in 1919 to promote World Revolution, it became after 1924 increasingly an arm of Soviet foreign policy. It is impossible to consider the development of Chinese communism without considering the relationship that it had with the Soviet Union.

There are then three key themes that will be considered in this chapter: the role of Marxism in the Chinese revolution; the impact of the national question on Chinese communism; and the role of the Soviet Union in Chinese politics.

2 The CCP from Formation to Power

In the early years of the 20th century it was increasingly apparent to many Chinese intellectuals that China would have to modernise, using Western methods, if it was ever to regain its political integrity. Intense political discontent led to the 1911-12 revolution, which overthrew the Manchu (Qing) dynasty. The revolution gave the presidency to Sun Yatsen, the founder of the nationalist party, the Guomindang (GMD). His party was based on the three Principles of the People. These were Nationalism, Democracy and People's Livelihood. By People's Livelihood Sun meant semi-socialist measures, such as the creation of state-owned enterprises, that would be the basis of Chinese prosperity.

Unfortunately Sun came up against two problems: the lack of either sufficient military support to sustain his position, or of any democratic tradition in China. To secure the abdication of the Qing emperor, Sun agreed to resign in favour of the ex-imperial general, Yuan Shikai. Once in power Yuan quickly made it clear that he had little interest in the principles of the GMD. He negotiated a large loan with a consortium of foreign powers in return for further territorial concessions and in 1916 had himself crowned emperor. After his death, later in 1916, China disintegrated even further, with large areas of the country coming under the control of independent military leaders, known as 'warlords'.

In 1917 another model of social transformation became available. Like China, Russia had been a predominantly peasant society ruled by an imperial autocrat. For some in China the Bolsheviks seemed to offer the way forward to a dynamic, modern society. Lenin's support for national self-determination and national liberation movements made his version of Marxism particularly appealing to the Chinese, enabling them to fuse Marxism with Chinese nationalism.

The newly formed CCP quickly attracted the attention of the Soviet leadership. Their perspective on Chinese conditions was that as the Asian proletariat was weak in general, all that could be hoped for in China was a national revolution led by the Chinese middle classes. Support for the national revolution, in alliance with the GMD, remained CCP policy until 1927.

Strangely, given their own recent history, the Russians imposed a very mechanical 'staged' notion of Marxism on the CCP. The justification for the identification of the middle class as the leading group in the national revolution was that China required a *bourgeois* revolution which, in turn, required a *bourgeois* leadership, as represented by the GMD. This, of course, was precisely the analysis of the Russian situation rejected by Lenin immediately prior to the October Revolution. This apparent contradiction can perhaps be explained by Stalin's struggle against Trotsky. From 1922 onwards Stalin and his allies adopted a series of policies that downplayed revolutionary action. This was the period of NEP, 'Socialism in One Country' and a policy of slow industrialisation (see page 63). The arguments over China thus became an extension of the arguments between the CPSU and Trotsky.

During the 1920s many CCP members were also members of the GMD. CCP members, including Mao Zedong, a founding member of the Party, occupied important positions within GMD organisations, and many thousands of CCP members participated in the Northern Expedition, a military enterprise to wrest control of territory from independent warlords. The Soviet government also offered assistance to the GMD: Soviet experts played a large part in its military academy and in its party organisation. Co-operation with the GMD did bring tangible benefits to the CCP. Party membership increased rapidly, as did trade union membership, under party leadership. This growth in influence disturbed many within the GMD who came from wealthy middle-class backgrounds. In 1926, in response to these tensions, Stalin ordered the CCP to curb peasant activity against landlords. Mao acknowledged these tensions in an article published in 1926, where he noted that a leading member of the GMD had written the following in a Peking paper:

> Raise your left fist to knock down imperialism and your right fist to knock down the Communist Party.[1]

This was a prophetic comment. Once it became clear that the Northern Expedition was going to be successful Chiang Kai-shek (Jiang Jieshi), leader of the GMD since Sun Yatsen's death in 1925, savagely turned on his erstwhile communist allies. In Shanghai, for example, the GMD executed up to 5,000 Communist Party members and sympathisers. Similar actions were carried out in other major cities. One effect of this anti-communist 'white terror' was to drive survivors out of the cities. This was to have a major effect on the course of Communist Party development, although this was not immediately apparent at the time.

Two years earlier Mao Zedong had become involved in the organisation of peasant unions. According to his own account the militancy of the peasants was something of a surprise: 'Formerly I had not realised the degree of class struggle among the peasantry.'[2] For the next two years Mao developed his views on peasant organisation, arguing for a radical policy of land redistribution and the organisation of the peasantry under Communist Party leadership. When, in response to the GMD's attack, leading CCP figures dispersed to the countryside Mao was one of the few who did so with detailed experience of political work amongst the peasantry. In 1930 the Party voted to establish a CCP (Soviet) government at Jiangxi. Although the leadership continued to talk about the leading role of the proletariat, the establishment of the Jiangxi government was part of a slow process of recognition of the real balance of forces in China. By the summer of 1930 there were over 100 Soviet districts, with a population of between 30 and 40 million. Three years later it was estimated that the Party had a total membership of 410,600, but only 60,000 of these were based outside Chinese Soviet territory. In the same year the leadership of the CCP transferred from Shanghai to Chinese Soviet territory, thus confirming the political reality that the CCP could only really operate in the rural areas of Southern China, protected by its own Red Army units. Despite this piecemeal acceptance of 'Maoism', Mao himself was, from 1931 to 1934, a somewhat marginal figure. Although the CCP and the Communist International had their disagreements about military strategy, they both tended to reject Mao's guerrilla approach.

At the end of 1934, the CCP was forced to evacuate its Jiangxi base. It was able to save face by claiming that it was going north to fight the Japanese. The Japanese had occupied Manchuria in 1931. This had caused considerable concern in Moscow as the Soviet Union shared a border with Manchuria. At the end of the year the Communist International had called for 'a national revolutionary war to oppose Japanese imperialists'. The desire to fight the Japanese was not, though, simply a pretext for the CCP's departure, for, as we have seen, many Chinese were attracted to the CCP precisely because of its opposition to imperialism.

The main body of the CCP left Jiangxi in October 1934, thus beginning the 'Long March' to China's remote North West districts. At the end of the 'Long March' the CCP and the Red Army established a secure base in Yanan province. Once there the Party continued the process of reorientating its policy to one of national defence against Japanese aggression. Although Mao and his forces were well beyond the reach of the Communist International, this 'national turn' was very much in line with the International's policy. At the Seventh World Congress of the Communist International, it was declared that the political choice facing 'the masses' was 'not between proletarian dictatorship and *bourgeois* democracy, but between *bourgeois* democracy and fascism'.[3] Hence, the socialist revolution was off the agenda, replaced by the defence of democracy. This change of policy was motivated by the Soviet Union's desire to build alliances with non-socialist powers to protect itself from fascist aggression. Within such a perspective the conversion of the CCP into a military force engaging the Japanese was clearly to be welcomed. The logic of this new role for the CCP was an alliance with the GMD, the other major national force.

Here the CCP was to benefit from discontent within the GMD armies. Many in the GMD forces were unhappy that Chiang Kai-shek continued to regard the Red Army, rather than the Japanese, as his principal enemy. At the end of 1936 Chiang was kidnapped by one of his own commanders and handed over to the CCP. After some intense discussions an anti-Japanese alliance was constructed and Chiang released. From then until 1946 the CCP and the GMD were linked in an anti-Japanese United Front. This alliance is sometimes seen as a cynical ploy, as a move that enabled the CCP to present itself as a truly patriotic organisation.

In practical terms, the Red Army conducted a guerrilla war against the Japanese. Given the overwhelming military superiority of their opponents this, in reality, was the only viable approach for them. At the end of 1936 Mao summed up this approach as: 'Fight when we can win and run away when we cannot.'[4] On a strategic level the Red Army regarded the countryside as its base, and spoke of 'surrounding the cities from the countryside'. A central element of the Red Army's

The Long March

approach was to win the support of the peasants. Before the formation of the United Front with the GMD, the Red Army had dispossessed and executed landlords, and then redistributed their land to
the peasants. After their agreement with the GMD, they dispossessed
only those landlords who were pro-Japanese. They did, however, abide
by a strict code of behaviour in their dealings with the peasants. They
behaved very differently from most of the armies that the peasants
were familiar with, and this undoubtedly played a part in winning
peasant support for the CCP.

In 1940 Mao published *On New Democracy,* a work which outlined his
view of how China would make the transition from a semi-feudal,
semi-colonial status to a socialist society. Here Mao stated his belief
that this process would be undertaken by a broad cross-class alliance.
One of the elements in this alliance was to be the *bourgeoisie,* as represented by the GMD. Implicit within the idea of a class alliance was the
idea that the coming revolution would be a national, not a class-based,
event. The society that Mao described emerging from this revolution
would not immediately be socialist: it would be based on three distinct
economic sectors - a state sector, a collectivised agricultural sector and
a private sector.

The political practice and programme of the CCP in the first half of
the 1940s was essentially national in character, and designed to
placate the GMD. Significantly, however, Mao claimed, in the same
year that *On New Democracy* appeared, that it would serve as a model
for all revolutions in colonial and semi-colonial countries. By doing so
he was staking his claim as a new and original Marxist thinker, gener-
ating ideas that had a wide, if not universal, political significance. The
outlook of *On New Democracy* fitted in with the rather more pragmatic
outlook of the Russian leadership. At the end of the Second World
War Stalin urged the CCP to reach arrangement with Chiang kai-shek
and support a government under his leadership. Indeed Stalin was
still urging such an arrangement as late as 1948.

Mao Zedong and Chiang kai-shek met in 1945 and signed an agreement. However, mutual antagonism between the CCP and the GMD
made it impossible for this to last, and civil war resumed in 1946. The
GMD had larger armies and better weaponry, but they were defeated by
the same tactics that the Red Army had deployed against the Japanese.
The CCP had, for example, the overwhelming support of the peasantry.

> Many peasants were joining the Communists. The single most important
> reason was that the Communists had carried out a land-to-the-tiller
> reform and the peasants felt that backing them was the way to keep
> their land.[5]

The Red Army also employed flexible guerrilla tactics, avoiding set
battles and moving around towns rather than wasting time besieging
them. Their better quality leadership and their efficiency corroded
the morale of a GMD army that was riddled with corruption. During

the course of the civil war 1.75 million GMD troops surrendered to the Red Army.

Crippled by wholesale desertions and surrenders, and facing the loss of huge quantities of weaponry, the GMD effectively collapsed in 1949. Chiang kai-shek and his surviving followers fled to Taiwan. In October of that year Mao Zedong declared the establishment of the People's Republic of China. His strategy had brought the CCP to power, not at the head of a proletarian revolution, but through a process of military conquest by a peasant-based army. The next issue to be addressed is the nature of the ideology used to justify this approach.

3 The Development of 'Maoism'

During his time in Hunan province, Mao developed a five-point programme:

> 1 My programme there called for the realisation of five points:
> (1) complete severance of the Provincial Party from the Guomindang,
> (2) organisation of a peasant-worker revolutionary army, (3) confisca-
> tion of the property of small and middle, as well as great, landlords,
> 5 (4) setting up the power of the Communist Party in Hunan, independent
> of the Guomindang, and (5) organisation of Soviets.[6]

This programme encapsulates the key points of Mao's distinctive political strategy. Although he refers to a peasant-worker army, simply by dint of his rural location the great bulk of any force assembled would have to be made up of peasants. In 1927, the year that Mao was sent to Hunan, he published *Report of a Investigation into the Peasant Movement in Hunan*. Within that report there is a section entitled 'Vanguard of the Revolution'. This contains no reference to the proletariat at all; instead the role of 'vanguard' is given to poor peasants.

Mao's 1927 programme represents the point at which he began to reorientate Chinese communism towards the peasantry. There are a number of reasons why he might have done this. It might have been a simple recognition that peasants represented more than 80 per cent of the Chinese population. It might also have been a recognition that a return to the cities and, therefore, contact with the proletariat was not likely in the near future. It might also have reflected Mao's own peasant upbringing. Whatever the reason it was to have enormous consequences for the development of Chinese communism.

Mao's decision to form an army is also very significant, for, even if the initial role of such a force was defensive, the long-term implica-tion was that political advance would come through military conquest. According to Marx, the industrial working class was poten-tially powerful because of its relationship to the means of production. Such a class could paralyse society by halting production and, more significantly, could lay, with its knowledge of production techniques and processes, the basis of a new, socialist society. Peasants could not act in the same way, since they lacked the industrial muscle of the proletariat and their proximity to the means of production. Consequently, any peasant-led revolution must involve a process of conquest. The peasantry was not in place within the industrial plants, so they would have to capture them from outside. For Marx, political power ultimately derived from the relationship of a class to the means of production. For Mao, political power, as he put it in 1938, 'grows from the barrel of a gun'.[7] The kind of forces that Mao assembled in the late 1920s were not sufficiently well equipped to take on conventional armed forces in open battle; they therefore used guerrilla tactics (surprise attacks, sabotage, and rapid retreats). A peasant orientation, a military strategy for political conquest, and the use of guerrilla tactics - these are the three essential elements of the 'Maoist' road to political power.

One consequence of the 'Long March' was the establishment of Mao as undisputed leader of the CCP. At the beginning of 1935 the communist forces halted to hold a party conference. There Mao argued that the Party had been unable to defeat the GMD's last campaign because it had failed to 'expand guerrilla tactics'.[8] In other words, the Party had failed to follow his tactics. At the end of the conference Mao replaced Zhou Enlai as president of the revolutionary military council and was elected to the politburo of the Party, soon becoming its effective head. Mao became, in effect, head of the Party and the Red Army.

Another distinctive feature of Mao's politics was his attempt to combine Marxism and Chinese nationalism. In 1938 Mao declared:

> 1 A Communist is a Marxist internationalist, but Marxism must take on a national form before it can be applied. There is no such thing as abstract Marxism, but only concrete Marxism. What we call concrete Marxism is Marxism that has taken on a national form ... If a Chinese Communist,
> 5 who is a part of the great Chinese people, bound to his people by his very flesh and blood, talks of Marxism apart from Chinese peculiarities, this Marxism is merely an empty abstraction. Consequently the Sinification of Marxism - that is to say, making certain that in all of its manifestations it is imbued with Chinese peculiarities - becomes a
> 10 problem that must be understood and solved by the whole Party without delay.[9]

The emphasis here is very important. A Marxist such as Trotsky would no doubt agree that distinctive national features have to be taken into account in any political analysis. This is clearly shown in his *Whither Britain?* However, to claim, as Mao does, that in a Chinese context Marxism has to be 'imbued with Chinese peculiarities' is to move well beyond simply taking account of national characteristics. It is to argue that each nation requires its own 'Marxism'; it is to move to a position where nationalism has a higher priority than the class perspectives of Marxism.

A feature of the late 1930s and 1940s is the degree to which Mao increasingly became the fount of all political wisdom. In 1943 he was described in the Party press as 'the star of the Chinese people'. In 1945 the new party constitution declared that 'the Thought of Mao Zedong' was necessary to 'guide the entire work of the party'.[17] Here a number of things are evident. Firstly, the beginnings of a process that would turn Mao's interpretation of Marxism into an unquestionable orthodoxy and, secondly, the beginnings of the creation of the cult of Mao.

4 The Establishment of the PRC

On assuming power in 1949 the CCP had three principal areas of concern: creating a stable political settlement; building a modern industrial state; and developing a role for China on the international stage. It should be remembered, however, that there was considerable overlap between these three areas. For example, China looked to the Soviet Union for assistance with industrialisation and such aid was, inevitably, conditional upon acceptance of Soviet leadership in international affairs.

Initially the new Chinese government described itself as a People's Democratic Dictatorship. What it meant by this was that it was an alliance of classes that genuinely represented the national interest. Democratic rights were to be accorded to those who defended the nation and who, therefore, were truly 'the people', and denied to those classes that betrayed the national interest. This is how Mao expressed it in 1949:

> 1 Who are the people? At the present stage in China, they are the working class, the peasantry, the urban petty bourgeoisie and the national bourgeoisie. These classes, led by the working class and the Communist Party, unite to form their own state and elect their own
> 5 government; they enforce their dictatorship over the running dogs of imperialism and bureaucratic bourgeoisie, as well as the representatives of those classes, the Guomindang reactionaries and their accomplices … Democracy is practised within the ranks of the people, who enjoy the rights of freedom of speech, assembly, association and so on. The
> 10 right to vote belongs only to the people, not to the reactionaries.[10]

There are a number of points to note about this extract. Firstly, that the enjoyment of democratic rights was conditional, not absolute. The phrase 'at the present stage' implies, at the very least, that those accorded these rights in 1949 might not always have them. Secondly, those given the vote are those calculated to vote the 'right way'. Thirdly, it is not made entirely clear what is meant by 'leadership of the Communist Party'. Not surprisingly, the political settlement of 1949 reflected these ambiguities. China was to be ruled by the Central

People's Government Council, which was established by the People's Political Consultative Committee. The Committee was made up of members of a variety of parties, but the Central People's Council they elected was entirely dominated by the CCP, eventually being made up of 56 leading Party members. The People, as defined by Mao, may have formed the government, but it was essentially a CCP government that was created.

During the period of the People's Democratic Dictatorship members of the middle classes who had worked under, or for, the previous regime, were encouraged to remain at their posts. This could be interpreted in two ways: either as a recognition that China was simply not ready for socialism, and had first to experience a *bourgeois-democratic* revolution, or that it was simply a pragmatic move to enable the CCP to establish their grip on state power. Given the relatively short duration of this period, the latter view seems more likely. In a public statement, *On People's Democracy*, issued in 1952, Mao declared:

> 1 Our present task is to strengthen the people's state apparatus - meaning principally the people's army, the people's police and the people's courts - thereby safeguarding national defence and protecting the people's interests. Given these conditions, China, under the leadership of the
> 5 working class and the Communist Party, can develop steadily from an agricultural into an industrial country and from a New Democratic into a Socialist and, eventually, Communist society, eliminating classes and realising universal harmony. Such state apparatus as the army, the police and the Courts are instruments with which one class oppresses
> 10 another. As far as the hostile classes are concerned, these are instruments of oppression.[11]

This statement effectively signalled the end of the People's Democratic dictatorship, as 'the instruments of class oppression' swung into action against what Mao called 'the bureaucratic capitalist class'. Political parties that had been tolerated since 1949 now disappeared in great campaigns against counter-revolutionaries and imperialists, terms that were defined as and how the CCP required. In the countryside the campaign against the landlords was intensified, the vast majority were expropriated and their holdings distributed to the peasantry. An untold number, possibly a million, lost their lives.

Whatever China's constitution, it was clearly ruled by the CCP, sustained, in the last resort, by the People's Liberation Army (PLA). In 1956 the CCP openly acknowledged that such was the case:

> As we have said before, the cause of socialism in our country cannot do without the dictatorship of the proletariat which is realised through the leadership of the Party of the proletariat - the Communist Party.[12]

At the same time as admitting CCP rule, China claimed to be a democracy. Since 1954 its supreme legislative body has been the elected National People's Congress (NPC). However, the fact that between 1954 and 1966 the NPC met only once a year gives some indication of the limited role it performed. Also, socialist democracy, as defined by the CCP, was a very different political construct from Western democracy. A Chinese statement of 1956 declared:

> The sole aim of socialist democracy, in the political, economic and cultural fields alike, is to strengthen the socialist cause of the proletariat and all the working people, to give scope to their energy in the building of socialism and in the fight against all anti-socialist forces.[13]

According to this definition, socialist democracy cannot be a vehicle for political opposition. Its role is to involve the mass of the population in the building of a socialist society, as defined by the CCP; it was not a system designed to allow the expression of a multiplicity of political beliefs. The limitations of Chinese democracy were made clear in the Hundred Flowers campaign of 1957. Using the slogan 'Let a hundred flowers bloom, let a hundred schools of thought contend', Mao initiated a movement of popular criticism against the state bureaucracy. Yet when it became apparent that the criticism unleashed was going far beyond acceptable boundaries, and even involved complaints against Mao himself, it was quickly stopped. Those who had been most active in the campaign were labelled 'rightists', subjected to criticism and, in some cases, expelled from the Party.

5 China's Economy

In 1952 the Chinese government announced that the first Five Year Plan for the economy was to begin the following year. This was closely modelled on Stalin's first Five Year Plan. Like Stalin's, it focused principally on heavy industry. Production targets were set for the coal, steel and petrochemical industries. Significant growth was achieved, and some authorities have suggested an overall growth rate of 9 per cent per annum. However, in specific industries the growth rate was much lower. Coal production, for example, only grew from 113 million tonnes in 1952 to 115 million tonnes in 1957. At this rate China would only develop very slowly into a major industrial power.

The problem was that the conditions obtaining in China were very different from those in Russia in the 1930s. Using the collectivisation of agriculture Stalin had reduced the agricultural workforce and placed agricultural production under state control. This enabled him to increase both the industrial workforce and squeeze sufficient produce out of the collective farms to feed this new workforce. In China the industrial workforce did increase, by over four million between 1953 and 1957. However, in the same period agricultural employment increased from 222 million to 297 million. This increase in the rural population meant that the capacity of Chinese agriculture to produce enough to feed an increasing industrial population was slight, and certainly it could not produce a surplus which might be exported to earn foreign currency. The problem was further compounded by the concentration of the Five Year Plan on heavy industry. This meant that there was only a very limited quantity of consumer goods available. Chinese farmers therefore had little incentive to increase production for the urban market because there was very little for them to buy.

Mao's solution to the relative failure of the first Five Year Plan was the initiative known as the Great Leap Forward (GLF). This was a typical example of his voluntarism, that is the belief that anything can be achieved if sufficient effort and willpower is expended. This attitude is clearly apparent in the slogan 'Capable Women Can Make a Meal Without Food'! Embedded within this is the belief that applied effort can always overcome adverse material circumstances. The GLF was described as 'walking on both feet'. This meant that agriculture was to advance at the same pace as industry. As part of this process all agricultural holding were reorganised into communes, containing an average of 20,000 people. Large-scale collectivised farming in the communes was seen as the way to increase agricultural production. Another element of the GLF was the mobilisation of China's vast population in the industrialisation process. Communes, schools, hospitals and universities were encouraged to build small 'backyard furnaces' to produce steel. By October 1958 over 600,000 such furnaces had been constructed.

The GLF mobilised the entire Chinese population in a frantic dash for economic growth. The result was disaster. The peasants, the vast majority of the population, who were forced to work increased hours in the fields and to work at their furnaces as well, were exhausted. Within the communes the compulsion to eat in communal mess halls, where the food was often inadequate, sapped their morale. The loss of control over their land and the removal of their equipment negatively affected their motivation to work. Production fell alarmingly.

1 ... food output fell from 250 million tons in 1958 to 150 million tons in 1959. In 1960 it fell by another 12.6 per cent and by 1962 it was a further 2.4 per cent down. In 1961 industrial production fell by 38 per cent and in 1962 by a further 16.6 per cent. Twenty million workers lost their jobs
5 and were sent back to the villages. More than one hundred million people suffered malnutrition.[14]

A drop in agricultural production meant a fall in the number of industrial workers who could be fed. Consequently it is not surprising that the GLF failed to meet most of its industrial targets as well. Most of the steel produced in the 'backyard furnaces' was of very poor quality and largely unusable.

The failure of the GLF was, in many ways, a personal defeat for Mao. He gave up the presidency of the PRC, although he retained his chairmanship of the CCP, and he appeared less frequently in public. In the early 1960s it fell to Liu Shaoqi, President of the PRC, and the CCP General Secretary, Deng Xiaoping, to restore China's badly damaged economy. This they did by slowing the rate of industrialisation and reintroducing an element of private farming. In some areas private farming accounted for over a third of the value of all produce. Mao did not like these retreats, but for the time being he could do nothing.

6 The PRC and the USSR

In the immediate aftermath of the formation of the PRC, Mao announced that the new republic would lean towards the Soviet Union in foreign relations. In the context of the developing 'cold war' it was not surprising that the new communist power should make that decision. Within a year of its formation the PRC was heavily engaged in a war with predominantly American forces in Korea. There were, however, also positive features to China's international alignment. Under the terms of the Sino-Soviet agreement of 1950 the Soviet Union undertook to provide China with loans and 10,000 Soviet technical advisers. Yet Sino-Soviet relations were not untroubled. Clearly fearful of the development of a potential challenge to Soviet leadership of the communist world, Stalin sought to exercise tight control over the PRC. The Chinese, on the other hand, remembered only too clearly that Stalin had supported the GMD right up to the end of the civil war. They disliked the fact that Soviet aid came in the form of high-interest loans, which had to be repaid; and they also disliked the reluctance of Soviet experts to share their knowledge.

Relationships significantly worsened in 1956 when Khrushchev delivered his secret speech denouncing Stalin, who had died in 1953, to the 20th Congress of the CPSU. Many of Khrushchev's comments there, like the following, could equally well be applied to Mao:

> ... quite a lot has been said about the cult of the individual and about its harmful consequences. After Stalin's death the Central Committee began to implement a policy of explaining concisely and consistently that it is impermissible and foreign to the spirit of Marxism-Leninism to elevate one person, to transform him into a superman possessing supernatural characteristics akin to those of a god ...[15]

In this context it is worth noting that many of Mao's writings from the 1930s and 1940s were rewritten after 1949, to eradicate the possible impression that he had ever made an incorrect decision.

Chinese unease about the nature of de-Stalinisation was confirmed by Khrushchev's announcement of the policy of peaceful co-existence with the capitalist powers. The Soviets argued that, in a nuclear age, the doctrine that war was inevitable with the capitalist states implied mutual destruction and so made no sense. The Chinese perspective, however, was that a nuclear war would simply result in the destruction of imperialism and that, therefore, there was no need to come to terms with the capitalist/imperialist powers, principally the United States. This disagreement reached a climax in 1960 when Khrushchev denounced the Chinese as 'madmen', anxious for nuclear war. In the same year he withdrew all Soviet experts from China. From that point on the CCP increasingly regarded the Soviet leadership as 'revisionist', that is guilty of revising away the revolutionary content of Marxism. This opinion was further confirmed by Khrushchev's 'capitulation' to the Americans in the 1962 Cuban missile crisis. Now the Chinese began to present themselves as the defenders of orthodox Marxism and the legitimate leaders of the world communist movement. Two key problems limited their effectiveness in this role: firstly, the distinctive methods of the peasant-based Chinese revolution offered little in the way of concrete guidance to Western communists, living in developed industrial states. Also, China's small industrial surplus meant that it could offer only very limited assistance to radical movements in the Third World. China's international revolutionary leadership was, therefore, largely of a rhetorical nature.

7 The Cultural Revolution

The Great Proletarian Cultural Revolution, an assault on pre-communist culture launched in 1966, can be interpreted in two ways. Mao's supporters argue that it reflected Mao's faith in the idealism of youth, his desire to combat the growth of a self-seeking and parasitic bureaucracy, and a wish to rejuvenate China's revolutionary spirit. His opponents interpret it as Mao's drive to reassert his absolute authority within China, by destroying the authority of the Party with a mass mobilisation of youth. What is beyond dispute is that the failure of the Great Leap Forward had weakened his position. Liu Shaoqi, who had replaced Mao as president of the PRC, declared that the economic problems of the early 1960s were 'due 30 per cent to natural disasters and 70 per cent to human errors',[16] a remark that clearly implicated Mao.

The Cultural Revolution had a slow build-up. It began with attacks on Khrushchevism. These were, in reality, veiled attacks on Mao's opponents within the CCP, in particular Liu Shaoqi, who had called Mao's authority into question, just as Khrushchev had questioned Stalin's. In 1965 Mao and his supporters attacked a playwright whose work, it was claimed, defended a disgraced opponent of Mao's. The Cultural Revolution properly took off in 1966 with the launch of the campaigns against the four 'olds': old culture, old thoughts, old customs and old habits. China's young people, organised into Red Guard units, were unleashed on these targets. In their campaigns ancient buildings and artefacts were destroyed; party leaders throughout the country were demoted, beaten, imprisoned and even killed; and the whole country turned against itself with people denouncing those around them in order to avoid being denounced themselves.

The Cultural Revolution is one of those events that can best be understood by looking at its consequences rather than the pronouncements of the protagonists. Between 1966 and the early 1970s the processes of production, the functioning of government and intellectual life were severely disrupted. One historian has claimed that up to 30 million people died as a consequence of the Great Leap Forward and the Cultural Revolution. Deng Xiaoping and Liu Shaoqi, the party leaders responsible for reversing the policies of the GLF, were removed from office and disgraced. The only organisation not disrupted by the Cultural Revolution was the People's Liberation Army (PLA). Indeed, it was the PLA that published millions of copies of *The Thoughts of Chairman Mao Zedong*, the 'little red book' that the Red Guards carried everywhere, and quoted ad nauseam. During the course of the Cultural Revolution the cult of Mao rose to new heights: he became the object of irrational and hysterical veneration for millions of Red Guards, well reflected by the following which appeared in the paper, *Red Flag*.

I O, most beloved chairman Mao, you are the Red Sun in our hearts. We cheer every day and sing every day. There are many intimate words we want to say to you. There are many songs we want to sing to you from the bottom of our hearts. All words of praise in the world may be
5 exhausted, but they cannot do full justice to your wisdom and greatness.[17]

His image also appeared on all major buildings. In the light of these consequences it is difficult not to conclude that the purpose of the Cultural Revolution had been to remove Mao's opponents and establish his absolute rule. When the Cultural Revolution looked like getting out of hand Mao ordered millions of young people into the countryside. The pretext for this move was Mao's belief that everyone could learn from the harsh realities of peasant life. However, the removal of 12 million young people from the towns was a very useful way of dispersing potential troublemakers.

By the early 1970s Mao's position was unassailable. But what had he created? China lacked any form of organised popular democracy. Even the 'democracy of the street protest' could only take place with the authorities' approval. When Zhou Enlai's funeral turned into a protest meeting, implicitly against Mao, it was forcibly dispersed. Mao could always, in the last resort, call on the forces of the PLA to deal with any movement he opposed. His person, image and writings were revered to a degree that went beyond the rational. In these circumstances it is not surprising that many Chinese dissidents likened Mao to the Chinese emperors of the past.

8 After Mao

Within two years of Mao's death in 1976, his old opponent, Deng Xiaoping, was in effective control of China's fortunes. Deng's approach to economic reform was essentially pragmatic, summed up in the phrase he had first coined in the 1960s: 'It does not matter whether a cat is black or white, so long as it catches mice.' In 1978 the Central Committee of the CCP accepted Deng's programme of 'four modernisations'. What this meant in practice was the restoration of market economics within China; the establishment of Special Economic Zones (SEZs) where private enterprise would predominate; and the introduction of a large element of private enterprise in agriculture. The results of these reforms were spectacular, and where once China sought to export revolution, she now exported manufactured goods. In 1991 Chinese exports were worth $71.9 billion, compared to $9.8 billion in 1978.

Economic reform, however, did not go hand in hand with political reform. The CCP, backed by the PLA, continued to rule China. The political attitudes of China's leaders were made only too clear in 1989, when the pro-democracy protest in Tiananmen Square, Beijing, was brutally suppressed by the tanks of the PLA. China today is a peculiar mix of old-style CCP leadership and Western free-market economics. Whatever else it might be, it is not a model for socialism.

Poster of Mao

9 Conclusion

By the end of the 1950s political power in China was concentrated in the hands of the CCP. The definition of democracy that operated within the country was such as to preclude political opposition. The CCP could not claim to have won power through popular democratic bodies - soviets - as the Russian communists could. The socialist society that the CCP began constructing in the 1950s also bore no resemblance at all to the visions of Karl Marx. In his account of the Paris Commune, which he regarded as a model for socialist societies, Marx noted, with approval, the abolition of the standing army and its replacement with a workers' militia; the election of political leaders by universal suffrage, immediately removable by popular vote; and the payment of the same wages to officials and workers. Quite clearly none of these conditions applied to Communist China. In 1953, for example, the civil service was divided into 26 grades. The pay for those on the lowest grade was one-twentieth of that of those on the highest. A worker's grade also determined a whole variety of other privileges: a high-grade worker, for example, would be entitled to a woollen coat, whereas a low-grade worker would only be entitled to a cheap cotton coat. Ultimately, also, as Mao implicitly acknowledged in 1952, the power of the CCP rested on the strength of the PLA, a standing army. This in turn reflected the fact that the Party had come to power as part of a process of conquest.

Mao clearly had enormous prestige within China. Obviously the cult of his personality was grotesquely inflated, but popular veneration was based upon a recognition of his role in taking China from imperialist domination to world power status. The same cannot be said for his supporters during the Cultural Revolution. They were quickly removed from power after his death, tried and imprisoned. This indicates one of the great weaknesses of Mao's version of socialism, that it focused so much on the role of one individual. Mao came to power as a result of the victory of the Red Army, later known as the PLA. As we have seen, he believed that political power came from the barrel of a gun. Once in power Mao was content to rule using his personal power, sanctioned, ultimately, by the barrels of many guns. In the aftermath of victory Mao did not create organs of popular democracy, like soviets. It is true that elected congresses were established, but, as we have seen, they rested on a very limited notion of democracy. In China socialism did not mean the empowerment of the population, it meant obeying orders. One Chinese dissident characterised Mao's approach as follows:

1   Marx wanted the workers to crush bureaucracy and replace it with democracy, and the Bolsheviks followed him in this. But Stalin and Mao simply replaced the old bureaucratic system with a new one - the Communist bureaucratic system. True, this new system was the
5 inevitable product of the turmoil of the October Revolution. But

whereas for Lenin it was a bitter fruit, for Stalin and Mao it was a delicious one.[10]

In the economic sphere China faced severe difficulties. Its peasant-based economy clearly could not create the society of plenty that socialism was supposed to be. China's economic situation was an objective fact that was clearly not Mao's personal responsibility. However, because of the lack of democratic restraint Mao was able to impose policies that significantly worsened the situation, like the Great Leap Forward. In a command economy economics and politics are closely intertwined; and if political power is largely concentrated in one pair of hands, a single wrong decision can have disastrous results.

Mao's pretensions, however, extended well beyond the boundaries of China. From the early 1960s the CCP claimed a leadership role in the international communist movement. What is undoubtedly true is that a number of movements in the Third World appear to have been influenced by Mao's road to political power. The Cuban revolution of 1959 very closely resembles Mao's, in that it involved the capture of the cities by a guerrilla army based in the countryside. The Vietnamese, in their long struggle against the French, and later the Americans, were also clearly influenced by Mao's principles of guerrilla warfare. However, it is important to note that most regimes that came to power using 'Maoist' methods nevertheless lined up with the Soviet Union, not China, a reflection no doubt of the relative abilities of those powers to provide economic assistance. However, even in the peasant societies of the Third World 'Maoism' has had very limited success. The same is true of China's attempt to win formal leadership of the communist world. The only state to line up with the Chinese - in the sense of accepting their ideological leadership - was Albania. Neither was the CCP able or willing to construct anything comparable to the Communist International. 'Maoist' organisations were established around the world, but their influence was slight, and they had largely disappeared by the 1980s. Given that Mao's version of Marxism was a 'Sinified' doctrine, it is not surprising that it did not travel well.

Finally, it is necessary to ask: was Mao a Marxist and should the PRC be described as a communist society? Of course it is necessary to keep in mind that practical politics will inevitably lead to the modification of political theories. Lenin clearly adapted Marxism quite considerably, and no one disputes his claim to be a Marxist. The question is, did Mao's adaptation go so far as to abandon essential elements of the doctrine?

References
1   Mao Zedong, 'Analysis of the Classes in Chinese Society', in *Selected Works of Mao Zedong Vol 1* (Lawrence and Wishart, 1954), p. 14.
2   Edgar Snow, *Red Star Over China* (Left Book Club, 1937), p. 157.
3   *Report of the Seventh World Congress of the Communist International,* August 1935.
4   Mao Zedong, 'Strategic Problems of China's Revolutionary War', in *Selected Works of Mao Zedong Vol. 1*, p. 244.
5   Jung Chang, *Wild Swans* (Flamingo, 1993), p. 129.
6   Snow, *Red Star Over China*, p. 163.
7   Mao Zedong speech 6th Nov. 1938 *Selected Works of Mao Zedong Vol. 2* (Foreign Languages Press, 1965), p. 224.
8   E.H. Carr, *The Twilight of the Comintern 1930-1935* (Macmillan Press, 1982), p. 373.
9   Stuart Schram, *Mao Tse-tung* (Penguin, 1975), p. 220.
10 James R. Townsend, *Political Participation in Communist China* (Univ. of California Press, 1969), p. 67.
11 Michael Lynch, *The People's Republic of China since 1949* (Hodder and Stoughton, 1998), p. 20.
12 Townsend, *Political Participation in Communist China*, p. 71.
13 Ibid., p. 78.
14 Gregor Benton (ed.) *Wild Lilies Poisonous Weeds. Dissident Voices From People's China* (Pluto Press, 1982), p. 41.
15 Nikita Khrushchev, *Speech to the 20th Congress of the CPSU* (24 Feb. 1956).
16 Benton, *Wild Lilies Poisonous Weeds*, p. 21.
17 *Hung Ch'I* (Red Flag), 1 Oct. 1966.
18 Gregor Benton, *Wild Lilies Poisonous Weeds*, p. 23.

Source-based question on 'Mao and China'

1. The nature of Chinese 'democracy'
Read the extracts on pages 92 and 93.
a) Who ultimately decides: 'who are the people'? What are the limitations of the form of democracy described in this extract? (p. 92) (6 marks)
b) According to this extract how are 'classes to be eliminated' (p. 93, line 8)? (4 marks)
c) What is meant by the use of the term 'dictatorship of the proletariat' (p. 93, line 2)? (3 marks)
d) Use all three extracts and information from the rest of the chapter to describe the key features of Chinese democracy. (7 marks)

Hints and Advice
a) According to this account 'the people' are not made up of the entire population. They represent a selection from the population. The question 'who makes the selection?' is crucial because only those selected will enjoy democratic rights. What the ques-

tion is really asking is whether this is democracy at all.

b) The extract does not answer the question directly but it does describe two processes, both of which relate to the treatment of classes hostile to the CCP. The question requires you to make explicit that relationship.

c) This question implies that the term as used in the extract has a hidden meaning. The question can be approached by breaking it down into key components. What, for example, was the proletariat and what role did it play in China? Was China a dictatorship? Who, or what, exercised power, if it was a dictatorship?

d) One way of approaching this question is to cross-reference terms that occur in all of the extracts. For example, the terms 'working class' and/or proletariat are used in all of them. What do they mean in this context? Don't forget that you are also required to support your conclusions with references to material in the rest of the chapter.

Answering Essay Questions on 'Mao and China'

1. Did Mao successfully adapt Marxism to Chinese conditions?
2. Was the Cultural Revolution really a campaign against 'old culture'?
3. What was the impact of the Great Leap Forward?
4. Mao argued that the Chinese Revolution was a model that could be followed by other Third World countries. Did this prove a realistic view?
5. Is the current People's Republic of China recognisable as the entity created by Mao?

Question 1 needs some careful discussion in the introduction. A great deal hinges upon the definition of success. Clearly Mao claimed to be a Marxist and, equally, he was successful in that he and his party achieved power. Another way of defining success is in terms of his attachment to Marxism. Did he successfully adapt it, or did he so fundamentally change it that it ceased to be Marxism at all? Having discussed the two possible definitions, you can then divide your essay into two sections discussing each of them and their relative significance.

Question 2 clearly implies that there was a hidden agenda to the Cultural Revolution. A good approach is to outline what it was supposed to do, what it actually did, and who benefited from it. In the section dealing with what it actually did you should consider which individuals and organisations did, or did not, suffer. This approach should lead to a conclusion that suggests the real motivation for the Cultural Revolution.

Question 3 falls logically into four sections. Why was the GLF started, that is, what was the context within which it was framed? What was it supposed to do? What did it actually do? What were the social, economic and political consequences of its implementation?

For the next question, it is necessary to identify the key, distinctive features of the Chinese Revolution. Secondly, you need to identify political movements that have adopted the Maoist model for their revolution. Then, on the basis of your second section, you need to discuss the applicability of the Chinese model of revolution for other states.

The final title is, in essence, a compare and contrast question. To answer it you have to identify the key features of the People's Republic of China, as established in 1949. You then have to consider how far China has, since 1976, retained or departed from the guiding principles of the state set up by Mao and the CCP.

Summary Diagram
Mao and China

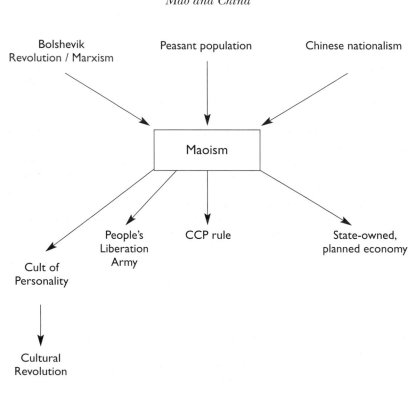

6 Socialism in the Post-Second War World

1 Introduction

At first sight it might appear that the period 1945-1956 was an extremely good one for socialists. In Britain Labour was elected into office with its first-ever outright majority. In Eastern Europe communist regimes were established from the Baltic to the Adriatic. In the aftermath of the German defeat socialists and communists occupied prominent positions in the newly elected democratic governments of Western Europe. Yet in reality things were much more complex. Many Western socialists were deeply disturbed by the way the socialist governments of Eastern Europe were formed. To many of them, it seemed that, with the exceptions of Albania and Yugoslavia, these new states were the creation of the Soviet Red Army, rather than the popular will of their peoples. Consequently, as the ideological differences between the Soviet Union and the United States developed into the Cold War, many Western socialists lined up with the United States because it seemed to embody democratic values in a way that the Soviet Union and its satellite states did not.

The Cold War further polarised attitudes between democratic-socialists and communists in the West. In Britain, for example, a number of communist sympathisers were expelled from the Labour Party. Western communists were further marginalised by their opposition to American aid for reconstruction, given as part of the US-funded Marshall Plan. The very success of Western socialists created problems for them. The British Labour Party, for example, in 1945 had for the first time won a substantial middle-class vote. This raised a number of questions. Had these middle-class voters been converted to socialism? If they had not and if such voters were essential to achieve power, did Labour have to change to retain their loyalty? The answers to these questions would have a fundamental impact on the development of reformist socialist parties throughout Western Europe.

The idea of a general socialist advance in the second half of the 1940s has to be considered in the light of three crucial factors. Firstly, that the socialist regimes of Eastern Europe were, in most cases, imposed by an external power, the Soviet Union. Many Western socialists were repelled by the actions of the Soviet Union in Eastern Europe. Any attempt to break from the Soviet bloc brought savage reprisals in the form of military intervention. This happened in Hungary in 1956 and Czechoslovakia in 1968. This led many Western socialists to line up with the United States against the Soviet Union. Domestically it led them to distance themselves from their national communist parties.

Secondly, Western communist parties, for instance in Italy and France, found themselves pulled in two directions. During the war it had been possible to combine support for the Soviet Union with national patriotism. In the Cold War period that was no longer possible. Initially these parties maintained their loyalty to Moscow, and lost much of the support they had built up during the war, so that the membership of the CPGB, for example, never exceeded its wartime peak of 55,000. From the late 1950s onwards these parties adopted an increasingly independent outlook, stressing their national roots rather than their Soviet affiliations.

Thirdly, reformist socialists continued to wrestle with the thorny problem of the democratic mandate. This was particularly so because people would vote for socialists *without* wishing for socialism. In the face of this discovery the reformist parties, the social democrats in Europe and Labour in Britain, had to decided which was more important to them: socialism or political power. The vast majority opted for political power and set to work modifying their politics accordingly.

To outline how these factors operated in practice the rest of this chapter will be divided into three sections. The first will look at the Labour Party in Britain, as an example of reformism in action; the second will look at the Italian Communist Party (PCI), one of the largest in Western Europe; and the third will consider the nature of Eastern European socialism.

2 The Labour Party

Labour's electoral triumph in 1945 was very much the product of wartime conditions. Between 1939 and 1945 a new set of political values were espoused by all of the major political parties, a development born of the need to maintain the morale of the British people. It was felt that they had to be promised a better life after the war than they had experienced before. Consequently, many of the measures that formed part of Labour's welfare legislation after 1945 first saw the light of day under the wartime coalition government, of which Labour was a part. This was true of Labour's social security legislation, which was largely based on the Beveridge Report, published in 1942.

In the 1945 election campaign the Conservatives, like Labour, promised to create a national health service; to intervene in the economy to avoid 'the disastrous slumps and booms from which we used to suffer'; and to maintain 'a high and stable level of employment'.[1] As the Conservative-dominated governments of the inter-war years had made no attempt to achieve any of these objectives, these commitments represented a considerable move to the left by the Conservatives. At the same time Labour moved significantly to the right. When discussing the issue of nationalisation Labour's 1945 manifesto declared:

> Each industry must have applied to it the test of national service. If it serves the nation, well and good, if it is inefficient and falls down on its job, the nation must see that things are put right.[2]

Here nationalisation ceases to be a question of principle, securing for the workers 'the full fruits of their labour', and becomes instead a question of efficiency. Two things flowed from this. Firstly, it committed Labour to a mixed economy, that is an economy consisting of both state-owned and private industry. Secondly, if nationalisation was simply a measure for dealing with inefficient industries, it could be discarded if it failed in that objective.

The full significance of this development only became apparent after Labour was defeated in 1951. During its time in office Labour had passed a large number of major pieces of legislation. They had created, among other things, the National Health Service. They had also nationalised a number of major industries, including coal and rail transport. During their 13 years in office (1951-1964) the Conservatives left the welfare state intact and did not launch a programme of wholesale privatisation. The two parties also had much in common on the foreign affairs front. When Labour first came to power in 1945 there was much talk of a more relaxed relationship with the Soviet Union, 'Left', it was said, 'would talk with Left'. In the event Labour played a major part in the creation of the anti-Soviet North Atlantic Treaty Organisation in 1949. Britain's perceived national interest played a much greater part in shaping Labour policies than any belief in fraternal, international socialist relations.

3 Labour Revisionism

A second general election defeat in 1955 produced a flurry of new thinking within the Labour Party, which was subsequently labelled 'revisionism'. The 'revisionists' argued that traditional class-based socialist policies were no longer relevant. Capitalism was no longer subject to violent economic fluctuations and could be managed by government without wholesale nationalisation; industries, it was argued, were increasingly run by professional managers rather than owners, and this rendered them more susceptible to government guidance in the national, rather than the individual's, interest. According to Anthony Crosland, a leading 'revisionist':

1 Traditionally, or at least since Marx, socialist thought has been dominated by the economic problems posed by capitalism: poverty, mass unemployment, squalor, instability, and even the possibility of the imminent collapse of the whole system. These were problems of the most
5 severe and urgent character; and it was correct to argue that major economic changes must precede the execution of socialist policy in other fields.
    But it is gradually ceasing to be correct to-day. Capitalism has been reformed almost out of recognition. Despite occasional minor reces-
10 sions and balance of payments crises, full employment and at least a tolerable degree of stability are likely to be maintained.[3]

Since, according to the 'revisionists', the major economic problems of capitalism had been solved, Labour should turn its attention to other, ethical issues, in particular equality, social justice and personal freedom. Reforms had to be secured within the existing economic system to achieve these objectives. Comprehensive education, for example, was seen as a key element in the drive towards the creation of a more equal society.

Another element in revisionist thinking was the belief that socialist policies, in particular nationalisation, were unpopular with the middle class. This perception no doubt played a large part in Hugh Gaitskell's decision, after being elected party leader in 1955, to try to get rid of clause 4 of Labour's constitution. This was the clause that appeared to commit the Party to wholesale nationalisation. Speaking at the Party Conference of 1959, in the aftermath of Labour's third general election defeat since the war, Gaitskell declared:

1   It [Clause 4] lays us open to continual misrepresentation. It implies that
    common ownership is an end, whereas in fact it is a means. It implies
    that the only precise object we have is nationalisation, whereas we have
    in fact many other Socialist objectives. It implies that we propose to
5   nationalise everything ...[4]

Gaitskell failed in his attempt to remove the existing Clause 4, but his objective, defined by one of his supporters as 'giving the party a more modern appearance and a stronger appeal to the uncommitted voter',[5] effectively set Labour's agenda down to the present day.

This agenda was certainly evident in the political rhetoric of Gaitskell's successor, Harold Wilson. In the 1964 general election campaign, Wilson identified the principal problems facing Britain as out-dated attitudes and inefficiency. This was an appealing approach to take as it ignored the question of class and promoted a theme that everybody could agree with. Who, after all, could be against national efficiency? If this was how Wilson defined socialism, who could disagree with it? At the same time as this rather bland socialism for the 'uncommitted voter' was being promoted, more traditional, and therefore contentious, elements of Labour's heritage were being downplayed. The two governments that Wilson presided over between 1964 and 1970 introduced only one nationalisation measure, and that was for the renationalisation of the steel industry. The Labour leadership also attempted to distance itself from the trade union movement. In 1969 the government issued the White Paper *In Place of Strife*, which proposed placing legal constraints on the actions of trade unionists.

By the time the Wilson government fell in 1970 certain key features of post-war Labour socialism were clearly visible. Post-war Labour promoted itself as a national, not a class, party. It is true that Labour leaders as far back as the 1920s had said the same thing, but the consequences of such an approach were not fully apparent in Labour's short-lived minority governments in the inter-war period. It also became clear that Labour saw socialism as the managing of an efficient mixed economy, and not as the planning of a largely state-owned economy. In elections, Labour tended to focus principally on the 'uncommitted voter'. This necessarily meant shaping their politics to the assumed preferences of the floating voter, jettisoning elements of its socialist heritage along the way.

These developments did not go unchallenged. As we have seen, Gaitskell failed in his attempt to drop Clause 4. Similarly, a still powerful trade union movement was able to force Wilson to abandon the proposals contained in *In Place of Strife*. Indeed, it is possible to see the period from 1970 to the mid-1980s as one long battle between Labour's modernisers and its traditionalists. Ironically, it was Labour movement defeats that made possible the victory of the modernisers. The growth in unemployment after 1979, and the defeat of the Miners' Strike of 1985, seriously weakened the trade union movement and undermined the scope for industrial militancy. Similarly, a succession of general election defeats (1979, 1983 and 1987) convinced many, and even some supporters of the left-winger Tony Benn, that Labour had to change fundamentally to become electable.

4 Victory for the Modernisers

The essence of the 'new realism' promoted by Neil Kinnock, elected leader in 1983, was that people's values had been fundamentally re-shaped by the free-market philosophy of the Conservatives under Mrs Thatcher. Consequently Labour could achieve power only by adapting to that development. Among other things, this meant accepting the market as the central governing mechanism of the economy, rejecting, that is, the idea of central economic planning. It also meant accepting that there would be no reversal of the 'Thatcher Revolution'. Tony Blair first came to public attention when, as shadow employment secretary, he announced that Labour would not reverse the Conservatives' anti-trade union legislation. What, according to Kinnock, made Labour distinctive from the Conservatives was its values.

> His [Kinnock] project was to provide a clear moral alternative to Thatcher's divisive vision of a harsh enterprise culture without any sense of community.[6]

Kinnock was rather vague on how a privately owned and competitive market economy would be invested with the values of 'community'; and, not surprisingly, some of his critics saw such talk as a cover for his move to the right.

Historically, however, Kinnock is likely to be seen as a staging post in the rise to power of Tony Blair, who, like Kinnock, also attempted to marry community values to the operation of the market. This is apparent within his rewritten Clause 4. One objective included in the new clause was for

1   ... a dynamic economy, serving the public interest, in which the enterprise of the market and the rigour of competition are joined with the forces of partnership and co-operation to produce the wealth the nation needs and the opportunity for all to work and prosper, with a
5   thriving public sector and high-quality public services, where those undertakings essential to the public good are either owned by the public or accountable to them.[7]

The original Clause 4 was seen by many as based on the labour theory of value, a belief that all wealth derived from the application of labour. This meant that those who produced the wealth should own the wealth. According to the new Clause 4, public well-being is to be sustained by the market economy, as a consequence of the profitability of a privately owned economy.

Given Blair's success in changing Clause 4, it is tempting to see him as the successful heir of the Gaitskellite revisionists of the 1950s. He certainly shares some key positions with them. Like them he supports the idea of a mixed economy; like them he has moved to abandon many of Labour's traditional ideological positions; and, also like them, he rejects class-based politics. However, Blairite Labour is also different in many ways from the earlier 'revisionists'. People like Crosland believed in equality, and promoted the idea of a taxation system designed to redistribute wealth from the rich to the poor; New Labour does not have such a policy. The 'revisionists' were also committed to a high level of welfare spending. New Labour is committed to reducing government spending, including welfare spending. The 'revisionists' were committed to government economic intervention to secure, among other things, full employment. New Labour is committed to reducing government economic intervention. One of the Chancellor's first actions, in 1997, was to hand over the control of interest rates to the Bank of England. These differences have led some critics of New Labour to suggest that it has abandoned the objective of social equality, or, to put it more negatively, has accepted the continuation of inequality.

At the end of the 20th century it is difficult to perceive what is actually socialist about New Labour. Given its commitment to market economics, and its refusal to adopt policies to redistribute wealth, it is perhaps not surprising that one of its disaffected ex-members should describe it as 'a Conservative Party Mark 3'.[8] The evolution of the Labour Party is the product of a number of factors. Participation in electoral politics almost automatically involves compromise, as parties have to strive to achieve a mandate. In Labour's most successful general election, in terms of votes, in 1951, it gained slightly less than 50 per cent of the poll. In these circumstances it could be quite reasonably argued that the party lacked a mandate for fundamental change. Accepting office with a limited mandate necessarily means operating within the constraints of a capitalist economy. Over the years what was initially presented as a necessity became a principle: hence the open espousal by Blair of the free market. The Labour Party, like other social democratic parties, was established as a party of the working class. However, since the Second World War class identification has been in decline. The old heavy industries that were the basis of the traditional working class and the trade unions have largely disappeared. The growth of home ownership and affluence have also eroded class loyalties. These, then, were the factors that explain Labour's development.

With their growing commitment to the free market, social democratic parties, like the Labour Party, have placed an increasing emphasis on providing incentives for business and industry, and also maintaining high rates of profit. This has inevitably led them away from a commitment to very high rates of taxation for the rich; indeed they have committed themselves to lowering taxation for all sections of the population. This has also, consequently, led them away from a commitment to high levels of welfare spending, funded by taxation.

> Bound by their interventionist traditions they [the social democratic parties] found it hard to redefine the relationship between the market and the state. Moreover, it was hard to reconcile the individualism of the market with the traditional social democratic ethos of social solidarity.[9]

Many within the Labour Party believe that they have solved the contradiction between market individualism and social solidarity. It is this belief that makes New Labour a model for European social democracy, and gives Blairism its historic significance.

5 Italian Communism

The communist parties of Western Europe were, from their foundation, intimately bound to the Soviet Union through their membership of the Communist International (Comintern). Though originally a source of pride, this connection was increasingly seen as a liability in the post-war period. From 1935 almost continuously through to the 1980s, communist parties had been at pains to stress their national, as opposed to international, affiliations. Up to 1939, this had been part of the Popular Front strategy, when the parties attempted in their various countries to establish broad anti-fascist alliances, including even non-socialists, to defend existing democratic institutions and, indirectly, the Soviet Union. During this period socialist revolution was definitely off the agenda. A very similar orientation emerged in 1941, after the Nazi invasion of the Soviet Union. During the war Communists in occupied Europe played a large part in national resistance movements. In Britain and the United States communists applied themselves to increasing production for the war effort. Of course such activities assisted the Soviet Union's war effort as well. At that time, therefore, it was possible to be pro-Soviet and patriotic.

Yet, despite communist rhetoric about their democratic and national loyalties, many non-communists throughout Europe in the post-war period, particularly with the onset of the Cold War, regarded the communist parties as simply the agents of Moscow.

This was the problem that confronted the Italian Communist Party (PCI). The PCI grew rapidly from 1943, the year of Italy's surrender, reaching a membership of 2.3 million by 1948. This rapid growth was in large part the product of the PCI's very active role in the anti-fascist resistance. From 1943 onwards the Party worked in a broad political alliance with a variety of parties, the largest of which was the Christian Democrats. In the first post-war election, in 1946, the PCI gained 4,360,000 votes, compared to 8,100,000 for the Christian Democrats. Leading figures from the PCI entered the centre-left coalition government that was subsequently formed. At this time the PCI was committed to the reconstruction of the pre-fascist democratic state. The PCI may, through the ranks of the anti-fascist partisans, have had access to large amounts of arms, but it nevertheless rejected the option of armed revolution; this was in line with the policy being promoted by the Soviet leadership. In 1943 they had wound up the Comintern as proof of their commitment to the Western allies and their rejection of revolutionary action.

Despite measures of this kind the West, and especially the Americans, remained deeply suspicious of Communist motives. In 1947, following a visit to the United States by the Italian Prime Minister, the communists and socialists were expelled from the government. It was widely believed that their removal was demanded by the Americans, before they would advance economic aid under the terms of the Marshall Plan. As international relations worsened so European communist parties returned to more class-orientated politics. These two developments were closely connected. In 1947 the Soviet Union established the Communist Information Bureau (Cominform) as a part substitute for the Comintern. It included the Eastern European communist parties and the larger Western European parties, like the PCI. It was designed to ensure that international communism presented a united front to the Western powers. The Cominform made clear to the PCI that a vigorous response was expected to the ejection of the Communist ministers. The PCI organised a series of mass strikes, through the medium of the CGIL trade union federation. Despite this resort to direct action, the PCI remained committed to a national road to socialism through parliamentary measures. When their supporters looked like going too far, as they did in mid-1948 following an assassination attempt on the PCI leader Palmiro Togliatti, the Party moved to restrain them, thus defusing a potentially revolutionary situation.

The key problem for the PCI was how to promote itself as a democratic national party and maintain its loyalty to the Soviet Union. The problem was neatly encapsulated by two statements made by Togliatti in 1956. In the first, following Khrushchev's 'secret speech' denouncing Stalin at the 1956 congress of the Communist Party of the Soviet Union, a move widely regarded as signalling the beginning of a process of liberalisation, he declared:

> Within the Communist movement itself one cannot talk of a single guide, but of progress which is achieved by following roads which are often diverse.[10]

This was a clear endorsement of the idea of 'national roads' to socialism, and also a rejection of the Soviet model of socialist change. In the other statement he endorsed Soviet military action against the Hungarian uprising.

> When the guns of the counter-revolutionaries are in operation one must be on one side or the other of the barricades. There is no third camp.[11]

There is a clear contradiction between Togliatti's support for 'diverse roads' to socialism and his support for the military imposition of the Soviet model on the Hungarian people.

Between 1956 and 1972 the PCI resolved the problem of simultaneous loyalty to Moscow and to a national model of socialism by moving to a more critical position on the Soviet Union and by placing much greater emphasis on their national programme. In the 1950s and 1960s the European-wide economic boom moved the PCI to a position of critical support for the European Economic Community. It would clearly have been unwise to oppose an organisation that seemed responsible for the elimination of unemployment and for substantial increases in the standard of living. This, in turn, meant that the PCI increasingly accepted the possibility of real social advance within the framework of existing society. At the same time Khrushchev's 'secret speech' had severely damaged the reputation of the Soviet Union. It was revealed as the land not of socialist advance but of slave camps, purges, mass executions and shortages. In another comment on the 'secret speech' Togliatti played down the idea that Stalin was solely responsible for the shortcomings of the Soviet Union: he suggested instead that it was due to the 'limitations of Soviet democracy'.[12] In other words, it was not the man but the system that was at fault. The biggest indication of a change in the attitude of the PCI came in 1968, when it severely criticised the Soviet invasion of Czechoslovakia, a very different response from the uncritical support it had given to the invasion of Hungary a decade earlier.

In the 1970s the doctrine of 'Eurocommunism' emerged. This was particularly associated with the communist parties of Italy and Spain. It stressed the democratic and parliamentary orientation of those parties. In many ways this was not a new approach, but the increasingly critical positions adopted by Western communists towards the Soviet Union gave it new emphasis. In Italy a central plank of Eurocommunism was the 'historic compromise'. This was essentially the idea of a national government resting on the three principal political traditions in Italy: communism, socialism and Christian Democracy. It was a compromise between the parties of labour and the party of capital. The rationale for these policies was the belief that a government of the left, within the Western world, was always in danger from American-engineered military coups. The 'compromise' was, then, the product of a deep political pessimism. The PCI stressed its acceptance of Italy's role as part of the Western military bloc, and noted that those who refused to recognise such realities, like the Greek communists in 1945, went down to defeat. Consequently, a reform government had to rest on the broadest possible social base, including classes other than just the working class. Such a broad-based government would also prevent the polarisation of the nation by blocking the creation of a centre-right coalition. The government envisaged by the PCI would be essentially a national not a class-based formation.

Some critical commentators have also pointed to the relatively static position of the left's share of the vote as a more accurate explanation of this development. In 1946 the combined left vote (PCI and the socialists) was 39.7 per cent, in 1972 it was 36.8 per cent. An alliance with the Christian Democrats was, it was claimed, the only way the PCI could achieve power. One problem with this policy was that the PCI was vague about what would come out of it. There were, however, indications of what such a government would mean in practice. In the mid-1970s Italy was suffering from wage inflation. Wage increases had to be contained in order to keep the price of Italian exports at competitive levels. In the national interest the PCI threw itself behind an austerity programme. In 1976 a leading PCI member wrote:

1   When we speak of the necessary sacrifices the workers must accept in order to overcome the crisis, it would be erroneous to conceive of these sacrifices as 'concessions' to the capitalists and the government, as is sometimes done, or the 'price' of a supposed Communist
5   manoeuvre aimed at getting into the government at any cost. On the contrary, the sacrifices are necessary if the country is to extract itself from the crisis in a manner consistent with the interests of the workers, if the youth are to find jobs, if the living conditions of the people are to improve.[13]

The PCI, a party formed to abolish capitalism was in the 1970s telling its supporters to accept sacrifices to sustain a capitalist economy because their well-being depended on the prosperity of that economy. In fact, by the mid-1970s the PCI had become indistinguishable from the parties of European social democracy. Despite its name the PCI was clearly not a communist party in the sense that Marx had used the term.

The 'historic compromise' failed. The Christian Democrats were quite prepared to accept PCI support in a difficult economic situation, and they were no doubt happy to have the PCI using its influence in the trade unions to promote their austerity measures, but they were not prepared to admit it to the government. One reason for this refusal was the fear that it would fragment Christian Democracy. Another reason was the hostility of the United States to increased communist influence, as, to a very large degree, they continued to regard the changes in PCI policy as no more than a deception concealing the Party's real purpose.

Yet the failure of the 'historic compromise' did not change the general direction of the PCI's development. At its 18th congress in 1989 the Party voted for a series of measures which speeded up the process of change. The Party accepted that the market economy was a permanent feature of economic life and the only real measure of economic efficiency. The Party statutes dropped all references to communist pioneers like Lenin and Togliatti, and retained only one brief quotation from Marx. In the early 1990s the Party even changed its name to the Party of the Democratic Left (PDS), thus finally severing all connections with the movement established by the Bolshevik Revolution.

6 The Future for Western European Communism?

The development of Italian communism reflects the general development of Western European communism, for example in France and Spain. As early as 1935 these parties, following the lead of Moscow, abandoned many aspects of classical Marxism and became national-democratic in orientation. However, their continuing links with the Soviet Union blocked their acceptance as legitimate parties during the Cold War. After 1956 these parties progressively shed their loyalty to the Soviet Union and their residual attachment to Marxism. In the process they became more and more like social democratic parties. They became committed to the success of their existing capitalist economies and they increasingly attempted to appeal to the whole of society, rather than primarily to the working class. The collapse of Eastern European communism stimulated some of them to break completely with that tradition by changing their names. In Italy where for much of the post-war period the PCI was the largest party on the left, this is an approach that has at least the potential to work. In Britain, where the CPGB never seriously challenged the Labour Party, the Democratic Left, successor to the CPGB, is scarcely visible above the political horizon.

7 Eastern European Socialism

It is a mistake to regard the socialist states that were created in Eastern Europe as a uniform bloc. In Czechoslovakia, for example, the Communist Party had a substantial following before the Second World War, in 1947 commanding 40 per cent of the popular vote. In Bulgaria in 1944 the armed forces prepared for the arrival of the Red Army by hoisting red flags and abolishing army ranks. Other states, like Poland, with a long history of conflict with the Soviet Union, were actively hostile towards the Red Army. However, despite these differences one feature was common to all the Eastern European states, except Yugoslavia and Albania, and that was that they were the result of Soviet foreign policy. It should be noted, however, that Soviet dominance in Eastern Europe had been agreed between the principal allies, Britain, the United States and the Soviet Union, before the war ended.

Initially the governments set up in these states were coalitions involving a variety of parties. Attitudes changed as the Cold War developed. The Soviet leadership saw the Marshall Plan as an attempt to extend American influence using economic aid. The Soviet leadership responded by advancing the Two-Camp Policy. According to which the whole world was divided between the peace-loving Soviet bloc and the predatory imperialist bloc, under American leadership.

In 1948 in response to this perceived threat the Soviet leadership decided that they needed to exercise tighter control over the Eastern Bloc. Within a six-month period private property had been abolished throughout the Bloc, and single party communist governments installed. The important point about this transformation is that it had not been brought about by the peoples of those countries but by the clients of the Soviet Union backed by the power of the Red Army. This process was entirely contrary to Marxist doctrine, which argued that socialist transformation must be the act of a politically conscious working class. What happened was revolution from above, not below. This process led the dissident Yugoslav communist leader, Tito, to comment:

> Were the path they have taken to be followed, that is bringing liberation on the bayonets of the Red Army, which would really be enslavement of peoples in another form, the science of Marxism-Leninism would perish.[14]

The governments thus established in the late 1940s were based on the Soviet pattern. They were undemocratic, authoritarian and depended on the twin pillars of a bureaucratic party machine and an extensive secret police network. While the Soviet government derived some legitimacy as the heir of the October Revolution, these governments depended very largely on Soviet military might for their legitimacy. Following the Soviet orchestrated invasion of Czechoslovakia in 1968, the Soviet leader announced what became known as the Brezhnev Doctrine:

1   ... when external and internal forces hostile to socialism try to turn the development of a given socialist country in the direction of restoration of the capitalist system, when a threat arises to the cause of socialism in that country - a threat to the security of the socialist commonwealth
5   as a whole - this is no longer merely a question for that country's people, but a common problem, the concern of all socialist countries.[15]

Here Brezhnev was advancing a justification for Soviet military intervention in any of the Eastern European states. The decision as to what constituted a threat to socialism was to be the Soviet Union's. Hence just as the creation of those states was largely the work of the Soviet Union, so too was their continuation and their foreign policies. It seems likely that it was the attempt by the Hungarians to abandon their military commitments to the Eastern Bloc that provoked Soviet intervention in 1956. A threat to socialism was, therefore, in reality a perceived threat to Soviet interests.

Most of the countries of Eastern Europe were economically underdeveloped at the end of the Second World War. Even those people who distrusted the Soviet Union believed that their countries would at least experience economic growth under their new regimes. In the event, the experience was a mixed one. In the first 15 years after the war the economies of Eastern Europe did grow, and at a faster rate than the economies of the West. This provoked a real fear in the West that they would be outpaced. However, much of this growth took the form of the construction of basic heavy industries, which could be built by the use of masses of labour. Also, it is important to note that in this period the economies of Eastern Europe were geared to supplying the needs of the Soviet Union, invariably on a very unfavourable basis. In 1948, for example, the Soviet Union bought the greater part of the Bulgarian tobacco crop at such a low price that when they sold it on the world market, they undercut the Bulgarians by 35 per cent.

The emphasis on heavy industry also produced shortages of consumer goods. This in turn produced food shortages, as the peasants had no incentive to bring their produce to market. In many states the authorities responded with collectivisation campaigns, although these generally worsened the food situation as the peasants lost their incentive to apply themselves productively. Problems such as these helped to fuel large and often violent protest movements, such as occurred in East Germany in 1953, Poland in 1956 and Hungary, also in 1956. The authorities dealt with these using a combination of coercion and conciliation.

In the early 1960s there was a recognition that economic development had to take on a more technical and scientific character. This need was publicly recognised by the Soviet leader, Khrushchev, at the

1961 congress of the CPSU. It was in this area that the economies of Eastern Europe faltered. This new industrial turn required the development of very complex equipment and the application of a great deal of scientific and technical expertise. The Eastern Bloc proved unable to generate either in sufficient quantities. Consequently, in the more liberal years of the late 1960s and 1970s it turned increasingly to the West for such expertise and equipment. This was to prove a very unequal relationship. The ability of the Eastern Europeans to earn foreign currency was very limited. The manufactured goods they had available for export were invariably inferior to Western products. Consequently, the only way that their goods could compete was if they were cheap. This, however, had certain consequences for their populations. It meant that wages had to be kept low and that they could only have a limited access to those consumer goods marked for export. Some states borrowed heavily in the West, but, invariably, because of the difficulties they had earning foreign currency, they had problems meeting their repayment commitments. This was the case in Hungary and Poland in the early 1980s.

The centrally planned states of Eastern Europe had industrialised their respective economies. They had also brought about an improvement in living standards since the end of the Second World War. However, these economies were obviously inefficient and subject to a variety of blockages in the production process. They were relatively weak in the production of consumer goods, and they certainly did not produce the state of plenty for all which was supposed to characterise socialism. Many of the peoples of Eastern Europe were only too well aware, from the Western television programmes they could receive, that Western Europe was characterised by a state of plenty. Not surprisingly, an equation developed that linked prosperity to the free market economy and political democracy.

8 Collapse in Eastern Europe

In 1985 Mikhail Gorbachev became leader of the Soviet Union. He was committed to modernising and restructuring his country. As part of his programme he planned to withdraw from Eastern Europe. When it became clear that the governments of the Eastern Bloc could no longer rely on Soviet support, they simply collapsed. In the course of 1989 communism was abandoned in Poland, Czechoslovakia, Hungary, Romania, Bulgaria and East Germany. Even Albania and Yugoslavia, both outside the Warsaw Pact, the Soviet Union's military alliance, abandoned communism shortly thereafter, as did the Soviet Union itself in 1991. All of these states now began to espouse free market economics and, less successfully, political democracy.

The Eastern European states had been a product of the settlement agreed at the end of the Second World War. Their establishment was not the result of popular uprisings or electoral success. The Eastern

Bloc countries were shaped by the policies and requirements of the Soviet Union. In the last resort, they lacked political legitimacy with their own peoples. It might well have been possible for the peoples of Eastern Europe to live with the very limited political rights extended to them: after all, before the Second World War many of these states had had authoritarian governments. However, the post-war communist governments did not simply fail politically, they also failed economically. Despite an initial rise in production, after 1960 most of these states experienced low, and even declining, rates of growth. It also became apparent that the general standard of living was much higher in the West. If these governments practised socialism, it was of a very deformed nature and consisted simply of the state ownership of the economy. The lack of support from their own peoples was vividly demonstrated by the rapidity with which they collapsed once Soviet support was removed.

9 Conclusion

The first obvious conclusion that this chapter leads to is that around the world socialist parties are abandoning socialism. The only old-style communist governments that still survive, at the time of writing (1999), are Cuba, the People's Republic of China and North Korea. The first two have dramatically modified their economies to accommodate large elements of private enterprise, and the third is in a state of collapse. Commitments to economic planning are being replaced by an acceptance of the market as the ultimate economic regulator. Similarly, commitments to state ownership are being reversed, and large-scale state enterprises are either being privatised or forced to compete with private companies. Most socialist parties now think in national, not class, terms and are keen to distance themselves from any vestige of their radical past. The key question is: how is this to be explained?

Some commentators have seen these developments as the product of the inherent superiority of democracy and free enterprise. They argue that, in practice, this socio-economic system was able to deliver the good life for its citizens, while socialism could not. Whether the free market will continue to be seen as an unquestionable good, however, is debatable. It may well be that environmental concerns will lead to governmental restraints being placed on the operation of unregulated capitalism. However, that remains in the future.

Other commentators have argued that the collapse of communism and socialism was due to specific historical circumstances. All of the states that had communist governments were, in comparison to the West, relatively backward before communism was established. Russia, China and most of Eastern Europe were all predominantly peasant societies. They therefore lacked the basic economic infrastructure to build socialism. Another variant of this argument is the view that the communist collapse represented a failure of the idea of 'socialism in one country'. Since the 1920s Leon Trotsky had argued that individual states could not become islands of socialism within a predominantly capitalist world economy.

As with all historical questions, this one has no final answer. This is particularly true here as the processes described are still working themselves through. The world is still living with the consequences of these developments. Students must, therefore, make themselves aware of the various explanations that have been advanced, and at the same time be aware of their provisional nature.

References

1   *Mr Churchill's Declaration of Policy to the Nation* (Conservative Party, 1945).
2   *Let Us Face the Future. A Declaration of Policy for the Consideration of the Nation* (Labour Party, 1945).
3   C.A.R. Crosland, *The Future of Socialism* (Cape, 1956), pp. 151-29.
4   Michael Foot, *Aneurin Bevan 1945-1960* (Paladin, 1982), p. 638.
5   W.T. Rodgers, (ed.) *Hugh Gaitskell 1906-1963* (Thames and Hudson, 1964), p. 126.
6   Geoffrey Foote, *The Labour Party's Political Thought* (Macmillan Press, 1997), p. 328.
7   Alex Callinicos, *New Labour or Socialism?* (Bookmarks, 1996), p. 5.
8   The *Guardian*, 17 Jan.1996.
9   Stephen Padgett and William E. Paterson, *A History of Social Democracy in Post-War Europe* (Longman, 1991), p. 258.
10 Donald Sassoon, *One Hundred Years of Socialism* (Fontana, 1997), p. 262.
11 Ibid., p. 263
12 Ibid., p. 262
13 Ernest Mandel, *From Stalinism to Eurocommunism* (NLB, 1978), p. 138.
14 Josip Tito, *Yugoslav Fortnightly* 2 Nov. 1949.
15 Leonid Brezhnev in Gale Stokes (ed.) *From Stalinism to Pluralism* (OUP, 1991), p. 133.

Source-based questions on 'Socialism in the Post-Second War World'

1   *Socialism transformed*

a)   Read the extract on page 110 of this chapter and the extract on page 76, in chapter 4. What is the essential difference between the old and the new Clause 4 of the Labour Party constitution? (4 marks)

b)   Read the extract on page 114 of this chapter and the extract on page 30, Chapter 2. Which really uses 'communist arguments'? Give reasons for your answer. (4 marks)

c)   Read the extract on page 116 of this chapter. Why does Tito believe that acceptance of liberation brought by the Red Army would mean the end of Marxism? (4 marks)

d)   Read the extract from page 117. What does Brezhnev mean by the term 'the socialist commonwealth'? (2 marks). Why does Brezhnev differ so widely from Tito on the question of military intervention for political purposes? (6 marks)

Answering Essays on 'Socialism in the Post-Second War World'

1. Is it still possible, in the 1990s, to describe Labour as a socialist party?
2. How is it possible to explain the collapse of the Eastern European communist states?
3. Why did the Italian Communist Party (PCI) abandon communism?

You should begin question 1 by defining socialism. However, that alone would not be satisfactory because the Labour Party has always practised a distinctive form of socialism. It is vital for you to consult chapters 3 and 4. The bulk of your work will then consist of a comparison of Labour in the 1990s and Labour in the past. You could also usefully ask, as you approach your conclusion, was Labour ever a socialist party? Your essay must move step by step to a conclusion, which provides an answer to the question based on your discussion.

A good starting point for the second question is to ask: what was the immediate cause of the collapse of these states in 1989? This will immediately raise the question of the role of the Soviet Union in their formation. From an examination of their formation you can move to their political systems, their economies and the level of support they enjoyed from their populations. Your conclusion returns you to your starting point, with the difference that you have demonstrated the full context of the role of the Soviet Union, and how that related to the support those governments enjoyed, or not.

Question 3: firstly you need to identify the key features of the PCI's abandonment of communism. These were an espousal of democracy and a desire to distance themselves from the Soviet Union. Secondly you need to identify the points at which these processes began. Thirdly you need to discuss the relationship between them. In your conclusion you should discuss the relative importance of these factors.

Summary Diagram
Socialism in the Post-Second War World

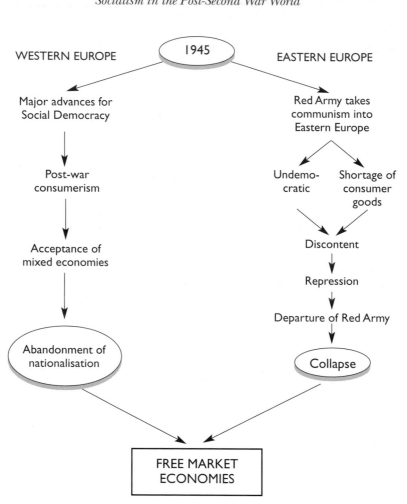

7 Conclusion: Socialism Past, Present and Future

At this point it is necessary to return to the issues raised in the introductory chapter. Here it should be possible to arrive at some answers to our initial questions.

a) What is/was Socialism?

Quite clearly socialism has taken a wide variety of forms. That said, it is possible to identify four basic elements that are present in the writings of socialist pioneers and later theorists. Firstly, it is generally agreed that the goods and services produced by any society should be equally available to all members of that society. It was this belief that led to the nationalisation of the economy becoming a socialist principle. The means of production should, it was argued, be owned by society so that the goods produced could be fairly distributed within society. Secondly, socialists have argued for the direct democratic control of social and political institutions. It was this belief that led figures such as Lenin and Marx to call for the replacement of professional armies by democratically controlled people's militias. In his 1871 pamphlet, *The Civil War in France*, Marx held up the Paris Commune as a model for future revolutionary governments.

1   The Commune was formed of the municipal councillors, chosen by
universal suffrage in the various wards of Paris, responsible and revocable at any time. The majority of its members were naturally working men, or acknowledged representatives of the working class. ... The
5   police, which until then had been the instrument of the Government, was at once stripped of its political attributes, and turned into the responsible and at all times revocable instrument of the Commune. So were the officials of all other branches of the administration. From the members of the Commune downwards, public service had to be done
10 at workmen's wages. The privileges and the representation allowances of the high dignitaries of state disappeared along with the dignitaries themselves.[1]

Thirdly, it was argued that the state control and planning of the economy within a modern socialist society would produce a state of material plenty. Finally, under socialism, the state would over time lose its coercive function. It was argued that in a state of material plenty, lacking class antagonisms, crime would largely disappear; consequently, the whole machinery of the police force, the legal system and the prison service would cease to exist. The state would, in that sense, disappear itself and be replaced by an administrative system to organise the distribution of goods.

The arguments that took place between socialists concerned the methods to be used to achieve these objectives. After 1917 this was primarily an argument between revolutionary communists and reformist social democrats. In the aftermath of the Bolshevik Revolution the argument moved to a different level. For many social democrats the undemocratic nature of the Soviet government demonstrated that revolutionary methods were counter-productive. It was not possible to separate the ends from the means. Brutal revolutionary methods, it was claimed, produced brutal undemocratic states.

b) Do Revolutions Always Fail?

It is impossible to escape the fact that all the socialist states created by revolutions have either collapsed or are experiencing severe economic and/or political difficulties. It seems reasonable to exclude most of the Eastern European states from this section, as they were not created by revolutions but by the military might of the Soviet Union, and they collapsed as soon as they lost that support. We are primarily concerned with the Soviet Union and the People's Republic of China (PRC), although the same points could be made about Fidel Castro's Cuba; all of these states were created by mass revolutionary movements and all of them were/are by Western standards profoundly undemocratic. It is important to note that all of these states were relatively backward and had to face the hostility and, in some cases, military intervention of the Western powers. That, however, is only part of the problem. Lenin once remarked that revolutionary parties only become mass parties on the eve of the revolution; but the problem was that of retaining mass support into the post-revolutionary situation. After the Bolshevik Revolution the Russian people experienced civil war, famine, forced industrialisation and the forced collectivisation of agriculture. They faced years of misery and suffering on an enormous scale. It could be argued that these experiences were inevitable in a backward state, but they certainly led to a loss of political support. However, having won power by force of arms, the Bolsheviks clearly were not going to throw in the towel in the face of adverse conditions. Instead they deployed coercion and repression, in the 'interests of the people', and the ultimate goal of full communism. The problem was that the Russian people were never given the opportunity to decide if the sacrifice was worth it, for the sake of this distant goal.

Revolutionary governments generally find it very difficult voluntarily to give up power. This is clearly demonstrated in the PRC. There seems little doubt that the Chinese Communist Party (CCP) has long since abandoned the goal of full communism. The development of free-market Special Economic Zones all along the coast of China and the preservation of Hong Kong's capitalist economy clearly shows this. However, as the bloody repression of the pro-democracy demonstrators in Tiananmen Square in 1989 demonstrates, the CCP leadership is definitely not prepared to concede political democracy, as this would obviously jeopardise its continuation in power. To date, no revolutionary state has either established popular democratic rule or a state of material plenty for its inhabitants. As a consequence such states generally lack long-term legitimacy with their populations.

c) Was Communism the same as Fascism?

Many commentators have noted the similarities between these two political systems. The both denied democratic rights, ruled through a single party and attempted to control every aspect of their citizens' lives. However, communist governments did destroy private ownership, whereas, fascist governments did not. The communist governments can, therefore, be seen as dictatorships that attempted to replace capitalism, whereas fascist governments attempted to preserve it. This key difference explains their mutual antagonism.

d) Was Marx Wrong?

Some Western Marxists take comfort from the fact that the collapse of communism took place in relatively backward states that were directly or indirectly the products of Stalinism. Such people argue that these states were not true reflections of Marxism in operation.

> We should forcefully remind people that Marx's political writings are democratic to the core, to the point where democracy is not an optional extra for socialists. Socialist structures must genuinely enable mass participation at every level.[2]

That may be the case, but what about Marx's views as to how his version of democracy was to be constructed? At the heart of Marx's analysis was the development of class consciousness. Revolution would occur, he argued, at the point when the working class became fully aware of its exploitation by the *bourgeoisie*. If, however, we consider the most advanced industrial states we find little evidence of this level of class consciousness. In Britain, the first industrial nation, communism has always been a marginal movement. At its peak in the Second World War, the Communist Party of Great Britain (CPGB) numbered only about 55,000. The party to which the bulk of the British working class has given its support in the 20th century, the Labour Party, was an explicitly non-revolutionary organisation.

One reason for this limited development of class consciousness would seem to be the ability of advanced capitalist economies to increase dramatically the standard of living of their populations, at least since the end of the Second World War. This runs counter to the Marxist belief that the need constantly to increase profits would lead to the progressive impoverishment of the working class. Marx, of course, was writing in the 19th century and, not surprisingly, his projections, based on trends then current, failed to predict the enormous expansive capacity of late 20th-century capitalism. As a result of this prosperity many within the working class tended to identify with capitalism, rather than seeing it as the enemy. Between 1945 and 1997, for example, the British Conservatives have been in government for 35 years, compared to 17 years for Labour. It would seem reasonable, therefore, to suggest that Marx was wrong on the relationship between capitalism and polit-ical-class alignments. Marx also claimed that capitalism, as a system, was inherently prone to regular economic crises. Here, it seems his views may still have some validity, as Eric Hobsbawm has recently argued.[3] The problems afflicting the 'tiger economies' of the Far East have severely dented the sense of triumph felt in the West at the collapse of communism.

It is interesting to note that in the post-war period, while revolu-tionary class consciousness has been at a low level in the industrialised states, successful revolutionary movements have appeared in the Third World. Some of the states established by these movements, like the Sandinistas in Nicaragua may have disappeared and others, like Vietnam, may have serious economic difficulties. However, their creation does point to one weakness of the capitalist system, and that is that on a global scale wealth is distributed in a very unequal fashion. It could, therefore, be argued that a global class struggle does exist between the developed 'have' nations of the West and the 'have not' nations of the Third World.

e) Is it Possible to be a Democratic Socialist Party?

This question arises from the fact that what distinguished the Western European social democratic parties from the communist parties of the east, was their commitment to electoral politics. It is interesting to note that the British Labour Party and the German SPD, which had very different origins, one as a Marxist party and the other as scarcely socialist at all, have both ended up in a very similar position advo-cating a kind of humanised capitalism. What both parties did have in common was a commitment, in practice, to electoral politics.

No reformist socialist party this century has managed to achieve an absolute electoral mandate. In other words, no such party has ever been in the position where it could say that the vast bulk of its pop ulation had voted for permanent and fundamental change. As a consequence of this, these parties tried to broaden their appeal, tried, that is, to win the votes of a broad section of their societies. This process can be seen at work in the last Labour Party leadership contest; a leading party member called for a leader who would:

> ... play best at the box office, who will not simply appeal to the tradi-tional supporters and customers of the Labour Party, but who will bring in those extra, additional voters that we need in order to win convinc-ingly at the next election.[4]

This process inevitably meant that their programmes tended to be national in scope, rather than purely orientated to the working class. A national programme also meant that such parties committed themselves to managing the national, capitalist economy. This can clearly be seen in practice. In the 1940s, for example, the Labour government used troops against strikers at least eighteen times, in the interest of the nation. From our perspective the principal consequence of the reformist approach is that such parties shape their policies in terms of the perceived views of a broad electorate. They do not, in other words, attempt to change popular opinion fundamentally. According to many commentators, Labour won the 1997 election because it abandoned those elements in its programme that clashed with the changes in outlook wrought by the Conservatives since 1979.

As no elected socialist government anywhere in the world has to date successfully introduced a permanent and fundamental socialist transformation, it would seem that electoral politics and socialism are incompatible. It would also seem that, therefore, the current developments within the social democratic parties represents a clear manifestation of their role to humanise, not to abolish, capitalism.

The term 'social democratic' has, since the end of the Second World War, come to refer to those socialist parties committed to managing mixed economies, rather than planning state-owned ones.

f) Is There a Future for Socialism?

This is the biggest question we have to address. It does need some refining though, before we can begin. Firstly, we have to separate communism and socialism. The communist regimes of the Soviet Union and Eastern Europe have collapsed but in Western Europe three major states, Britain, Germany and France, will enter the next century with socialist-led governments. This distinction in turn relates to the question of how socialism is defined, the point at which we started. There are those who would deny that social democracy and communism are variants of socialism at all. The problem with this view, often put forward by supporters of Trotsky's variety of Marxism, is that there are no governments that meet with their complete approval, and consequently it is impossible to test their conception of socialism in practice.

Despite these distinctions there are some comprehensive explanations offered for the collapse of all forms of socialism. The commonest of these is the view that socialism cannot work because it runs against the basic urges of human nature. People are, according to this view, inherently competitive, selfish and acquisitive; they are motivated, in other words, by qualities that run against the co-operative ideals that socialism seeks to embody. The problem with this view is that it is ahistorical and assumes that the characteristics that people display in free market economies are natural and have existed for all time. However, at the beginning of the Industrial Revolution there was considerable resistance to the application of free market (then called *laissez-faire*) economics; indeed, many early forms of socialism were attempts to embody the values of the past in a new form (see Chapter 2).

A more convincing general explanation is that all forms of socialism failed to develop a more effective mechanism for the distribution of goods and services than the free market. There certainly seems to be a considerable body of evidence to support this. All of the major social democratic parties have abandoned the twin ideas of nationalisation and direct economic planning for an almost complete reliance on the market as an economic regulator. Similarly, it can be argued that the states of Eastern Europe collapsed largely because they failed to adopt the free market. Hence, many Westerners see the fall of communism as the result of the triumph of the free market. However, another distinction has to be made here, and that is that the great majority of the communist regimes have disappeared while, although transformed, the social democratic parties of Western Europe appear to be prospering.

g) Conclusion

One obvious conclusion is that none of the movements and parties surveyed in this book have successfully introduced socialism, as defined at the beginning of this chapter. Indeed, those parties that survive are rapidly abandoning old-style, class-based socialism, as represented in the photograph below. This takes us back to the question: is there a future for socialism? It is always rash for historians to

Tony Benn sitting in front of The Workers' Union, Witney Branch banner.

make predictions. Our business is the past, not the future, however, it would seem reasonable enough to suggest that the very specific conditions that produced the two main currents of socialism in the 20th century - communism and social democracy - are very unlikely to reoccur. However, looking back at the past it also seems reasonable to say that throughout human history the unequal distribution of wealth has produced radical and indeed revolutionary movements. At the present point in time it seems safe to suggest that the unequal distribution of wealth, both domestically and globally, will continue. Indeed, it is possible to demonstrate that the parties of social democracy are actually committed to inequality.

Inequality is inevitable within a free market system, as those with higher incomes have access to a greater share of what is available. Most of the time, in the Western world, such inequalities are acceptable, mitigated as they are by a range of welfare measures. They might seem less acceptable if the number of 'safety nets' was dramatically reduced. Gross inequalities of income in the new free market economies of Eastern Europe, where welfare provision is often minimal, might well prove a catalyst for radical movements.

Ultimately, it is not possible to predict the nature of any future socialist movements. However, it is possible to agree with Neal Ascherson that all societies based on an unequal distribution of the good things of life have the potential to generate revolutionary movements.

1 Revolutions are always about the same things. They are always about unjust distribution of property, about political tyranny. They are about a mass impatience with the way of governments. This will happen again. And when it does, there will be some resemblances to the Bolshevik
5 Revolution. Some of its principles will always be here, like the dream of absolute equality. A lot of the conceptions are just too good to die. People will always strive for these things.[5]

References

1 Karl Marx, 'The Civil War in France', in *Karl Marx, Friedrich Engels Selected Works Vol. 2* (Progress Publishers, Moscow, 1969), p. 220.
2 Terry Eagleton, 'The Real Left Has No Need to Apologise', in *Stalinism, the Left and Beyond. A Symposium* (Workers' Liberty, 1992), p. 15.
3 Eric Hobsbawm, 'Markets, Meltdown, and Marx', The *Guardian* 20 Oct. 1998.
4 John Rentoul, *Tony Blair* (Warner Books, 1996), p. 357.
5 Neal Ascherson, 'Marx was Wrong about Class', in *Stalinism, the Left and Beyond* (Workers' Liberty, 1992), p. 8.

Source-based questions on 'Conclusion: A Future for Socialism?

1   Karl Marx on socialist democracy.
Read the extract from Marx on page 123.
a)   What do you think Marx meant by the phrase 'stripped of its political attributes' (line 6), when talking about the police? (4 marks)
b)   Why did Marx believe that it was necessary for officials to be paid the same wage as workmen? (4 marks)
c)   What did Marx mean by the phrase 'responsible and revocable instrument of the commune' (line 8)? (6 marks)
d)   Using information from the preceding chapters, compare this description of a revolutionary government with the historical reality of other socialist states.(6 marks).

2   The Workers' Union
Study the poster on page 128.
a)   What does this picture tell you about 'traditional' socialism? (5 marks)
b)   Compare the 'message' of the poster with the politics of New Labour. (5 marks)
c)   Why could it be argued that the images the poster contains are no longer relevant? (5 marks)

Chronological Table

1789	The French Revolution begins.
1797	Gracchus Babeuf, leader of the Conspiracy of Equals, was executed.
1824	Robert Owen established the socialist community of 'New Harmony' in the United States.
1827	First use of the term socialism in the Owenite *Co-operative Magazine*.
1833	Owen established the Grand National Consolidated Trade Union.
1840	Pierre-Joseph Proudhon published *What is Property?*
1845	Friedrich Engels published *The Conditions of the Class in England*.
1848	Karl Marx and Friedrich Engels published the *Communist Manifesto*.
1864	The International Working Men's Association (First International) was founded.
1867	Marx published the first volume of *Capital*.
1875	The Social Democratic Party of Germany (SPD) founded.
1876	The First International was dissolved.
1881	Russian *Narodniks* assassinate Tsar Alexander II.
1883	The first Russian Marxist group, the Group for the Emancipation of Labour, formed.
1884	The Social Democratic Federation, the Socialist League, and the Fabian Society were formed in England.
1889	The Socialist (Second) International established in Paris.
1891	The SPD adopted the (Marxist) Erfurt Programme.
1893	The Independent Labour Party (ILP) was formed in Bradford, England.
1898	Alexandre Millerand, an independent socialist, entered a *bougeois* French government.The Russian Social Democratic Labour Party (RSDLP) formed.
1900	Labour Representation Committee founded. In 1906 it took the name: Labour Party.
1903	The RSDLP split into the Bolshevik and Menshevik factions.
1905	The SFIO, French section of the Workers' International, was formed.
Aug. 1914	The First World War broke out. The great bulk of the Socialist International's membership disregard anti-war resolutions, and supported their national governments.
Feb. 1917	First Russian Revolution.
Oct. 1917	Bolshevik Revolution.

1918	The German Kaiser abdicated. The first SPD chancellor, Ebert, took office. In November revolution spreads throughout Germany. At the end of the year the Geman Communist Party (KPD) was formed.
	The British Labour Party adopted a socialist constitution.
1919	Communist International (Comintern) founded.
1921	The Chinese Communist Party (CCP) formed.
1922	Soviet government banned all political parties, except the Communist Party.
	Stalin became General Secretary of the Communist Party.
1924	The first Labour government came into office.
1927	Leon Trotsky expelled from the Soviet Communist Party and sentenced to internal exile.
	The Guomindang (GMD) savagely attack their former allies in the CCP.
1928	Stalin initiated the first Five Year Plan and the collectivisation of agriculture.
1929	The second Labour government elected.
1930	Last inter-war German SPD chancellor falls from office.
1931	The British Labour government fell as a result of the financial crisis. Fewer than 60 Labour MPs were returned in the Nov. General Election.
1933	The Nazis came to power. The SPD were banned.
1934	The CCP began the 'Long March'.
	The 'Great Terror' began with the assassination of Kirov.
1935	Mao Zedong became leader of the CCP.
1936	The CCP and the GMD formed anti-Japanese alliance.
1939	Germany and the Soviet Union signed a non-aggression pact.
1945	First majority Labour government elected in Britain.
1946	Civil war between the CCP and GMD resumes.
1949	The People's Republic of China (PRC) established.
1952	First Chinese Five Year Plan began.
1953	Stalin died.
1956	Krushchev made 'secret speech' at the 20th congress of the CPSU, denouncing Stalin's crimes.
	Anti-communist Hungarian uprising supressed by Soviet troops.
1957	Mao launched the 'Hundred Flowers campaign'.
1958	The 'Great Leap Forward' launched by Mao.
1959	Hugh Gaitskell attempted to remove Clause 4 from the Labour Party constitution.
1962	Cuban missile crisis produced rupture between the Soviet Union and the PRC.
1966	Cultural Revolution began in China.
1976	Mao died.

1977	Central Committee of the CCP accepted Deng Xiaping's modernisation programme.
1989	Massacre of pro-democracy protesters in Tiananmen Square.
	Communist governments of Eastern Europe collapse.
1991	The Soviet Union was dissolved.
1994	Tony Blair elected as leader of Labour Party.
1995	Clause 4 of the Labour Party's constitution rewritten.
1997	The Labour Party was elected into office.

Further Reading

There is a very large body of work covering this area. It would, there-fore, be impossible to provide a comprehensive reading list. Students wishing to read further should consult the bibliographies of the larger works referred to below, like, for example, Donald Sassoon, *One Hundred Years of Socialism* (Fontana, 1997). Students should also bear in mind that books in this area do not always fall into neat categories, and that some books will be relevant to more than one of the group-ings used here.

1 Socialism

Students should be aware that many authors include communism as a form of socialism in their books. George Lichtheim, *A Short History of Socialism* (Fontana, 1975) is a very useful book. It covers the develop-ment of socialism as a doctrine from the late 18th century to the mid-1970s. It also includes a very good bibliography. Edmund Wilson, *To the Finland Station* (Penguin, 1991) deals with the emergence of early 19th-century socialism, and the development of Marxism up to the the Bolshevik Revolution. Julio Alvarez del Vayo, *The March of Socialism* (Jonathan Cape, 1974) writes from a partisan socialist position, but his book does have the advantage of covering a long period, from the French Revolution to the 1970s, and also of looking at socialists outside of Europe.

2 Marxism

David McLellan, *The Thought of Karl Marx* (Macmillan, 1995) deals with the development of Marx's thought in a clear systematic way and contains a great many useful quotations. David McLellan, *Marxism After Marx* (Macmillan, 1980) examines the developments of various forms of Marxism from Marx's death through to the 1970s. There are also a number of useful short guides to Marx's life and works, including: Peter Singer, *Marx* (OUP, 1980) 82pp., and David McLellan, *Marx* (Fontana, 1986) 93pp. Alex Callinicos, *The Revolutionary Ideas of Karl Marx* (Bookmarks, 1996) is a lively, if partisan, work, which traces the development of Marx's ideas and argues for their continuing relevance.

Students should also attempt to read some primary texts. Karl Marx, Friedrich Engels, the *Communist Manifesto* (Penguin, 1992) is probably the most accessible introduction to the basic ideas of Marxism. V.I. Lenin, *The State and Revolution* (Penguin, 1992) is the classic defence of revolutionary political action.

3 European Socialism

Dick Geary, *European Labour Protest 1848-1939* (Methuen, 1984) is a very useful short work, 190pp., that discusses the conditions that led to the emergence of organised Labour movements in Europe. Dick Geary (ed), *Labour and Socialist Movements in Europe Before 1914* (Berg, 1989) contains essays dealing with the major European countries and Russia. Stefan Berger, David Broughton, (eds), *The Force of Labour* (Berg, 1995) contains essays dealing with the developments of labour and socialist movements in 20th-century Europe. Walter Kendall, *The Labour Movement in Europe* (Allen Lane, 1975) provides a comprehensive account of European socialist and labour movements from the late 19th century through to the post-Second World War period. Albert S. Lindemann, *A History of European Socialism* (Yale University Press, 1983) covers the period from the late 18th-century to the early 1980s. Perry Anderson, P. Camiller, *Mapping the West European Left* (Verso, 1994) is a collection of essays looking at left-wing movements in the major West European states since the Second World War.

4 Russia and Eastern Europe

Richard Pipes, *The Russian Revolution 1899-1919* (Harvill, 1997) gives a very detailed account, and provides a lot of information on the development of Bolshevism. Isaac Deutscher's three volumes of biography on Trotsky, *The Prophet Armed; The Prophet Unarmed; The Prophet Outcast* (OUP, 1970) contain an enormous amount of detail, although written from a pro-Trotsky perspective. Orlando Figes, *A People's Tragedy. The Russian Revolution 1891-1924* (Jonathan Cape, 1996) is a very detailed account that interweaves personal with more general material. Dmitri Volkogonov, *Lenin. Life and Legacy* (HarperCollins, 1995) a negative interpretation of Lenin's legacy, which Volkogonov argues lasted until the fall of communism. E.H. Carr *The Twilight of Comintern 1930-1935* (Macmillan, 1982) is a useful account of the Communist International under Stalin. Gale Stokes, *From Stalinism to Pluralism* (OUP, 1991) is a collection of documents dealing with Eastern Europe from 1945 to 1989. Gale Stokes, *The Walls Came Tumbling Down* (OUP, 1993) deals with the collapse of communism in Eastern Europe. Geoffrey Hosking, *A History of the Soviet Union* (Fontana, 1992) gives a comprehensive account of the Soviet Union from its formation to its fall. Michael Lynch's two volumes in the Access to History series are both very useful, *Reaction and Revolution: Russia 1881-1924* (Hodder & Stoughton, 1992), *Stalin and Khruschchev. USSR 1924-64* (Hodder & Stoughton, 1990).

5 France

Students should be aware that France is also covered in the material listed in the European Socialism section. Paul E. Corcoran, *Before Marx. Socialism and Communism in France, 1830-48* (Macmillan, 1983) is a useful collection of documents relating to French socialist pioneers. Tony Judt, *Marxism and the French Left. Studies on Labour and Politics in France 1830-1981* (Clarendon Press, 1989) is, as its title suggests, a wide-ranging study of French socialism. Tom Kemp, *Stalinism in France* (New Park, 1984) deals with the development of communism in France from the 1880s to the present day.

6 Germany

Again Germany is covered by the European section as well. Helga Grebing, *History of the German Labour Movement* (Berg, 1985) gives a clear concise account of German Labour from the early 1800s to the mid-1960s. W.L. Guttsman, *The German Social Democratic Party 1875-1933* (George Allen and Unwin, 1981) gives a dry, but thorough account of the SPD from its formation to its dissolution under Hitler. Sebastian Haffner, *Failure of a Revolution. Germany 1918/19* (André Deutsch, 1973) provides a very readable account of the 1918 revolution, and its significance.

7 Great Britain

Geoffrey Foote, *The Labour Party's Political Thought* (Macmillan, 1997) is a very useful book that deals with the whole of the party's history right up to the 1990s. James Hinton, *Labour and Socialism. A History of the British Labour Movement 1867-1974* (Wheatsheaf Books, 1983) provides a very good and concise history of the Labour movement. Ralph Miliband, *Parliamentary Socialism* (Merlin, 1972) gives a radical critique of Labour's attachment to parliamentary politics. Henry Pelling, *A Short History of the Labour Party* (Macmillan, 1978) is a very useful and concise account.

8 China

Michael Lynch, *China From Empire to People's Republic* (Hodder & Stoughton, 1996) and Michael Lynch, *The People's Republic of China Since 1949* (Hodder and Stoughton, 1999) together give a clear well-structured account of China's history from the beginning of the century to the present day. Stuart Schram, *Mao Tse-tung* (Penguin 1975) is a good basic biography of Mao, if rather uncritical in its approach. Stuart Schram (ed.) *Mao Tse-tung Unrehearsed. Talks and Letters 1956-71* (Penguin, 1974) is a good introduction to Mao, in his own words. Gregor Benton (ed.) *Wild Lilies and Poisonous Weeds. Dissident Voices from People's China* (Pluto Press, 1982) is another useful collection of primary material, this time from critics of China's government.

Index

New Economic Policy 63

Owen, Robert 5, 16-19, 20

Paine Tom 14
Paris Commune 123
Peoples Republic of China 1, 84,
    92-4, 119, 124
Poland 116, 117, 118
Proudhon, Pierre-Joseph 20-1

Ricardo, David 16
Rochdale Pioneers 18
Romania 118
Russia 6, 85, 119
Russia Social Democratic Labour
    Party 51, 54

Saint-Simon, Henri de 19, 20, 21
Sandinistas 126
Second (Socialist) International
    3, 7, 9, 37, 40, 53
SFIO (French Section of the
    Workers' International) 43,
    44, 53
Smith, Adam 14, 16
Snowden, Philip 76
Social Democracy 6, 7, 8, 10
Social Democratic Federation 45
Social Democratic Party 8
Social Democratic Party of
    Germany 1, 38, 39, 40, 53,
    58, 67-75, 126
Special Economic Zones (SEZs)
    99, 124
Stalin, Joseph 4, 6, 10, 31, 61,
    63, 65, 66, 80, 89, 94, 96
Stalinism 3
Sun Yat-sen 84
Socialist Workers' Party 32

Trotskyism 3, 4, 10
Trotsky 10, 31, 61, 63, 65, 91,
    127

Union of Soviet Socialist
    Republics (USSR) 1, 4, 9,
    10, 61, 66, 80, 84, 96-7, 105
    115-8, 124

Vietnam 6, 126

Warsaw Pact 118
Webb, Beatrice 10, 64, 65
Webb, Sidney 2, 10, 46, 64, 65
Wilson, Harold 108

Yugoslavia 116